Savoring
IRELAND

DEDICATION

For Louis, Eva, and Christine

ACKNOWLEDGMENTS

*I would like to thank Christine Cullen for her generous assistance in
preparing the manuscript and her helpful suggestions throughout the
work. I'd also like to thank Eveleen Coyle and Fleur Robertson for the idea
and for their confidence and patience, and my cooking friends and
colleagues for inspiration.*

EDITOR Fleur Robertson
AMERICANIZATION Beverly LeBlanc
CONSULTANT Kathleen M. Zelman
DESIGN Louise Clements
PHOTOGRAPHY © Michael Diggin Photography
RECIPE PHOTOGRAPHY © Quadrillion Publishing Ltd
PRODUCTION Ruth Arthur, Karen Staff, Neil Randles
DIRECTOR OF PRODUCTION Graeme Proctor

5040 Savoring Ireland
Published in 1998 by CLB, an imprint of Quadrillion Publishing Ltd,
Godalming Business Centre, Woolsack Way, Godalming, Surrey, England GU7 1XW
Copyright © 1998 Quadrillion Publishing Ltd
Distributed in the USA by Quadrillion Publishing, Inc.
230 Fifth Avenue, New York, NY 10001

Savoring
IRELAND
Cooking through the seasons

NUALA CULLEN

CLB

contents

introduction

THE VISION of ancient Celtic Ireland that has
come down to us through folklore and poetry is of a land
of plenty, where poetry and music were among the
important occupations of man, and honor and hospitality
went hand in hand.

Through the centuries, hospitality continued to be a matter of honor, with rich and poor alike. Nearer to our own times, in the eighteenth and nineteenth centuries, successive travelers to Ireland have invariably commented on the lavish welcome, the rich variety and quantity of food, and the large numbers of persons entertained. The ill-fated dependence upon the potato by almost a quarter of the population, however, and the tragic aftermath of the failure of the potato crop in the successive famines of the 1840s, is all too well known. Life changed profoundly for many people as a consequence and the tradition of prodigal hospitality was almost swept away. Ireland, however, is a natural food-producing country, and, in recent decades, extensive research has given an improved understanding of the best production methods for our food resources, producing a true land of plenty, with Irish products in demand all over Europe. There has been a renaissance in Irish cooking, too. Many country-house owners have opened their homes and tables to visitors. Kitchen gardens are being restored to their former splendor, their produce forming an

important part of the cuisine. There is, too, a new generation of Irish chefs, cosmopolitan in their training although with roots in their own tradition, who are creating a discernibly Irish style of professional cooking, which allows the excellent raw materials to speak for themselves. Modern storage methods have largely made the seasons redundant, removing, to some extent, the great pleasure of looking forward to the next month's delights. In most cultures, festival days, with their attendant seasonal foods, are the only bulwark against this. We are fortunate in Ireland that many of these feasts are still observed, even if only in perfunctory way.

The recipes included in this book aim to give an idea of some of the dishes particular to the seasons, foods that have been in common use in Ireland for many hundreds of years (with one or two exceptions), although using the latest modern methods. I hope you will enjoy them, and they will contribute in some measure to the enjoyment of your guests and the conviviality of the dinner table, a pleasure as important in Ireland today as it has been for centuries.

SPRING

IN NATURE'S calendar, the true new year begins in February when the first signs of growth appear and almost imperceptibly the days begin to lengthen.

As the year begins to unfold, the old festive days still punctuate the seasons, many of them associated with particular foods. St. Brigid has pride of place with her feast day, February 1, appropriate for such a powerful, near-mythical figure, patroness of dairying and brewing, and in whose honor reed or rush crosses were made to be placed on house doors and cow byres. They are still made today, although most likely to be found in craft stores. St. Valentine comes next and has laid claim to chocolate; and Shrove Tuesday, the day before the austerities of Lent begin, is a day when children still rush home from school to eat crêpes. St. Patrick, curiously, has no particular food association, although corned beef and cabbage on this day is popular with Irish Americans. The high point of the Christian calendar is, of course, Easter, with its spiced buns and cakes—these a tradition of great antiquity—and, of course, lamb. Its sacrificial symbolism did not mar the enjoyment of those who had abstained from meat for the six weeks of Lent. Eggs, now made of chocolate, but formerly painted and decorated hen's eggs, are given as presents and used in games. After Easter, life resumes its normal tenor, the days lengthening quickly as summer approaches with its promise of early vegetables and fresher, lighter food.

S P R I N G
a p p e t i z e r s

MUSSELS WITH BACON
AND RED WINE

"Lord Smart (to Neverout): Tom, they say fish should swim thrice.
Neverout: How is that, my Lord?
Lord Smart: Why, Tom, first it should swim in the Sea (Do you mind me?), then it should swim
in Butter; and at last Sirrah, it should swim in good Claret."
Jonathan Swift, *Polite Conversation*

4¹/₂ pints live mussels
6 slices bacon
1 cup red wine
2 tablespoons butter
1 fresh thyme sprig
4 shallots
2 garlic cloves, finely chopped
3 large ripe tomatoes,
  seeded and chopped
1 tablespoon all-purpose flour
2 tablespoons chopped
  fresh parsley
salt and freshly ground
  black pepper

Clean the mussels thoroughly, discarding any that are broken or don't close when sharply tapped. Put them in a large saucepan, with the wine. Cover, bring to a boil, and cook 2 minutes, shaking the pan from time to time, until the mussels are open.

Transfer the mussels to a bowl, discarding any that have not opened. Strain the liquid into a bowl, discarding any sand or grit.

Melt 1 tablespoon butter in a saucepan. Add the thyme and bacon and cook until crisp. Add the shallots and garlic and cook until soft. Add the tomatoes. Mash the remaining butter and the flour together and stir into the saucepan, a piece at a time, stirring until the flour is cooked and the sauce is smooth. Add the mussel liquid gradually, stirring until the sauce has thickened. If it is too thick, add a little water. Reheat the mussels in the sauce for a few moments. Stir in the parsley. Check and adjust the seasoning. Serve with fresh crusty bread.

Serves 6

Ruined village, Blasket Islands
Previous page: Co. Kerry smallholding

Spring

SPRING GREEN SOUP

Soups of this type were very popular in the past, providing much needed vitamins and minerals after a winter diet of dried legumes and winter roots. The ingredients can be varied according to which shoots have made their appearance or are available.

large handful of sorrel leaves
large handful of spinach
handful of young nettles or
   cultivated dandelion leaves
heart of a small green cabbage
4 tablespoons butter
2 onions, finely chopped
2 garlic cloves, chopped
chopped fresh thyme
2 potatoes, peeled and
   chopped
2¹/₂ cups chicken stock, or
   milk and water
²/₃ cup whipping cream
salt and freshly ground
   black pepper

Wash all the leaves thoroughly in salted water, removing any coarse stems or ribs; keep the nettles separate. Prepare the cabbage in the same way, shake dry and finely chop.

Melt the butter in a large saucepan. Add the onions, garlic, thyme, spinach, cabbage, and sorrel and sweat. Add the potatoes and the stock, or milk and water, and simmer until the potatoes are soft. Add the nettles and cook until they are tender, about 30 minutes. Purée, add the cream, adjust the seasoning, and serve.

Serves 6

SPICY CARROT SOUP

1 tablespoon oil
1 tablespoon mustard seeds
2 tablespoons butter
2 onions, chopped
4 to 5 large carrots, grated
1 tablespoon coriander seeds
5 cups chicken or vegetable
   stock
2 tablespoons oatmeal
1 tablespoon cider vinegar
juice and grated zest of 1
   large orange
salt and freshly ground
   black pepper
chopped fresh cilantro, to
   garnish (optional)
cream, to garnish (optional)

Heat the oil in a large saucepan and add the mustard seeds, heating until they pop. Add the butter and onions and cook on a low heat until they begin to soften. Then add the carrots and coriander seeds and continue cooking 5 to 6 minutes. Add half the stock and the oatmeal and cook a few minutes longer. If you like a smooth soup, purée the mixture at this point. Return to the saucepan, add the vinegar, orange juice and zest, and remaining stock. Season well. Simmer a few moments and serve.

The soup can be garnished with a swirl of cream and some chopped, fresh cilantro if you like.

Serves 6

Spring vegetable garden

SOUSED HERRINGS

The herring has been a staple of the Irish diet for centuries, and its seasonal appearance was greeted with pleasure by rich and poor alike. Huge fleets set out from Killybegs in Donegal in search of the "silver darlin's." Originally, sousing was a simple method of preserving surplus herring or mackerel, but it became a popular dish in its own right. The sousing liquid here is a mild version, and, if the herrings are to be eaten hot, leave them in the marinade for several hours, or overnight, to allow the flavors to develop. For a spicier flavor, add a little chili.

8 to 10 herring fillets
8 to 10 shallots
2 to 3 bay leaves
1 onion, sliced

FOR THE MARINADE
1¼ cups cider or
 white-wine vinegar
1¼ cups hard dry cider or
 white wine
2 teaspoons juniper berries,
 slightly crushed
ground dried chilies or
 fresh chilies, to taste
1 to 2 tablespoons each of
 brown sugar, mustard seeds,
 and black peppercorns

Boil the marinade ingredients together gently for a few minutes. Leave to cool and let infuse 30 minutes. Preheat the oven to 300°F. Lay out the fish fillets on a board and arrange a peeled shallot and a piece of bay leaf on each half. Roll up and secure with a wooden toothpick. Arrange in a baking dish. Strew the onion slices over the top and pour the marinade into the dish. Cover with foil and bake 30 to 40 minutes.

Cool before packing into a plastic box, large enough to let the cooking liquid cover them. Chill, overnight if possible. The herrings can be kept 2 to 3 days in the refrigerator.

Makes 8 to 10

OYSTERS WITH SPICY PORK PATTIES

St. Valentine's Day calls for something special: delicious, of course, with amorous associations, and not too much trouble. The old fashion of eating chilled oysters and chipolatas (tiny hot spicy sausages) with champagne or white wine seems ideal. Chipolatas may be difficult to find, so prepare and chill your own pork patties the day before and then cook them quickly, for 10 minutes or so, when required. Serve hot, alternating with the chilled oysters.

12 oysters, opened (see
 below), on the deep half of
 the shell
½ onion, finely chopped
1 garlic clove
2 tablespoons butter
¾ pound lean pork, finely
 ground
2 teaspoons Worcestershire
 sauce
1 tablespoon finely chopped
 fresh parsley
pinch each of dried thyme,
 grated nutmeg, and hot
 ground red chilies

Cook the onion and garlic in a little butter until soft. Chill before mixing with the pork, if the patties are being prepared in advance. Mix the meat with the remaining butter, sauce, parsley, and remaining flavorings. Stir in the onion and

garlic and mix thoroughly. Using floured hands, shape into small patties, about 1½ inches wide; they should be hot and spicy but not so much so they kill the taste of the oysters and wine. Cook them in a skillet, without any extra fat, about 10 minutes until cooked through.

Note: to open an oyster, hold it firmly in your left hand and insert a short, sharp knife near the hinge, working it from right to left until it begins to release. Prise open.

Serves 2

Ballybunion Castle, Co. Kerry

COD'S ROE AND COD'S ROE PÂTÉ

The season for cod's roe is very short, a mere 2 to 3 weeks between February and March, so it is important to make the most of it and, as the roes freeze well, either raw or cooked, it's a good idea to buy extra when they are available. If cod's roe is unavailable, substitute salmon, herring, or tuna roe.

To cook, simply tie the roe loosely in a plastic bag, cover with boiling water, and simmer slowly until it is firm to the touch. Leave to cool and remove from the bag. The simplest and most traditional preparation is to cut it into thick slices, dip in seasoned flour, or egg and bread crumbs, and fry slowly in a mixture of butter and oil until crisp. Serve for breakfast, with crisp bacon and broiled tomatoes or mushrooms, or for lunch with creamy mashed potato and a slice of lemon.

4 to 5 ounces cooked cod's roe
4 to 6 tablespoons butter,
  melted
juice and grated zest of
  ¹/₂ lemon
salt
cayenne or ground chili
  to taste
fresh chives, chopped

Purée all the ingredients in a food processor until smooth. Pack into ramekins and chill. This is delicious with hot toast, as an appetizer.
  Serves 4

Donkey plow, Co. Kerry

POTATO SOUP WITH SALMON AND CHIVES

This different potato soup includes the excellent farmed salmon available all year round.

6 ounce salmon, steak or
  tail piece
4 tablespoons butter
6 potatoes, peeled and
  chopped
2 leeks, chopped
1 onion, finely chopped
1 bay leaf
2¹/₂ cups fish or chicken stock
2¹/₂ cups milk
2 tablespoons finely chopped
  fresh chives
salt and freshly ground
  black pepper

Put the salmon in a small saucepan and just barely cover with water. Poach gently until the fish is cooked and flakes easily, about 10 minutes. Remove from the water, then skin the fish, remove bones, and flake; set aside. Add the water to the fish or chicken stock to make it up to 2¹/₂ cups.

Melt the butter in a large saucepan. Add the onion and leeks and cook until tender but not colored. Add the potatoes, bay leaf, stock, and seasonings. Bring to a boil and simmer until the potatoes are soft. Remove the bay leaf. Purée the soup in a food processor, then return to the saucepan. Add the milk, chives, and salmon and gently bring to a boil. Adjust the seasoning and serve hot.

Serves 6

S P R I N G
m a i n   c o u r s e s

HAKE BAKED IN PAPER

This method of cooking was widely used in the past to protect delicate morsels from the heat of the open fire. Baking parchment is the ideal material, sealing in the flavors and appearing somehow more aesthetic on the plate than foil. The fish can be served with a selection of roasted vegetables.

4 hake, cod, or whiting fillets, weighing 4 to 8 ounces each
4 tablespoons butter
1 large red bell pepper
chopped fresh dill or marjoram, leave some for garnishing
4 tablespoons dry vermouth or white wine
8 to 10 live mussels, to garnish
salt and freshly ground black pepper

Preheat the oven to 350°F. Cut 4 pieces of parchment large enough to enclose the pieces of fish.

Season and butter the fish well. Place one fillet on each piece of parchment. Slice the pepper into thin rounds, removing the seeds and white membrane and place 1 or 2 slices on top of each piece of fish. Sprinkle a pinch of chopped dill or marjoram on each and pour 1 tablespoon vermouth or wine over each piece of fish. Bring the 2 sides of the paper together and pleat lengthwise, tucking the ends firmly under the package to seal. Place the packages in a baking dish and brush with butter. Bake 20 to 25 minutes, depending on the thickness of the fillets.

Scrub the mussels well, discarding any that are not firmly closed. Steam the mussels open in a covered pan with a few tablespoons water; discard any that don't open.

When the fish is cooked, cut a slit in the paper with scissors and garnish with the mussels and remaining herbs. Serve; it is usual to allow each guest to open their own package but experience suggests it is best to make the initial incision first.

Serves 4

Tralee Bay, Co. Kerry

SALMON CAKES WITH DILL SAUCE

To make these fish cakes, use either a tail piece or cutlets or, better still, the buttery remains of a whole salmon.

1¹/₂ pounds salmon

3 tablespoons finely chopped shallot

6 tablespoons butter, melted

1 egg yolk

1 tablespoon lemon juice

1 tablespoon finely chopped fresh herbs

2¹/₂ cups fresh bread crumbs

1 tablespoon whipping cream, if necessary

1 egg, beaten

2 tablespoons each whole-wheat flour and dry bread crumbs, mixed

salt and freshly ground black pepper

butter and oil for frying

FOR THE DILL SAUCE

1 tablespoon butter

1 tablespoon all-purpose flour

1 cup milk, hot

3 to 4 tablespoons crème fraîche or sour cream

2 tablespoons finely chopped fresh dill or 2 teaspoons dried dill

salt and freshly ground black pepper

Poach the salmon in salted water 12 to 15 minutes. Remove any skin and bones and flake the flesh. Sauté the shallot in a little of the butter until softened. Mix the salmon, shallot, egg yolk, lemon juice, remaining melted butter, herbs, and seasonings together. Add the bread crumbs and work well together; add the cream if the mixture is too dry. Firmly shape into 4 or 8 fish cakes, using floured hands. Dip the fish cakes into the beaten egg and then into the bread-crumb-and-flour mixture.

Melt a little butter with the oil in a large skillet. Add the fish cakes a few at a time, if necessary, and fry 5 to 6 minutes each side until crisp. Drain on paper towels and keep warm until all the fish cakes are cooked. Serve with dill sauce.

To make the sauce, melt the butter in a saucepan. Whisk in the flour and stir until cooked, about 1 minute. Off the heat, gradually whisk in the hot milk. Bring back to a boil and stir until it thickens. Stir in the crème fraîche or sour cream and dill and season to taste.

Serves 4

Lough Carra, Co. Mayo

BUTTER BEAN HOT POT

This comforting dish is an example of the homely cooking we all love to return to. If dried butter beans are not available substitute dried lima beans.

1½ cups dried butter beans,
  soaked overnight
1-pound slab bacon, rind
  removed and flesh cubed
oil for frying
3 cups sliced onions
2 large sharp cooking
  apples, peeled and sliced
3 cups sliced potatoes
chopped fresh thyme
1 or 2 fresh sage leaves
1¼ cups vegetable stock
  or water
salt and freshly ground
  black pepper

Drain the beans and re-cover with fresh water. Bring to a boil and boil 10 minutes; then simmer until soft but not breaking up, about 40 minutes; drain and set aside.

Preheat the oven to 300°F. Brown the meat in a little oil in a heavy pan. Remove the meat and brown the onions in the same pan. Layer the onions, beans, bacon, apples, and potatoes in a greased ovenproof casserole. Sprinkle with thyme and pepper and tuck in the sage leaves. Finish with a layer of potatoes. Add a very little salt and pour the stock over. Cover with foil or a lid. Bake for about 2 hours.

Remove the foil and continue cooking until the potatoes are brown. Add a little more stock, if necessary. A simple green salad is good with this.
Serves 4

CHICKEN AND CHEESE
WRAPPED IN BACON

This simple dish uses the traditionally popular combination of chicken and ham, with the piquant addition of Cashel blue, one of Ireland's finest cheeses, which gives just the right note of acidity to the dish. Add a creamy blue cheese if Cashel blue is unavailable.

**4 boneless, skinless
  chicken breasts**
8 bacon slices
2 to 3 fresh sage leaves, torn
grated lemon zest
6 ounces Cashel blue cheese
2 tablespoons butter
**glass of white wine, vermouth,
  or chicken stock**
**2 to 3 tablespoons whipping
  cream**
**salt and freshly ground
  black pepper**

TO GARNISH
lemon wedges
fresh sage leaves

Place a chicken breast flat on a board and, with a sharp knife, slice in half horizontally. Cover each piece with plastic wrap and beat gently with a rolling pin until slightly larger. Cut each slice of bacon in half and stretch the pieces out by stroking with the blade of a large knife. Lay 2 pieces of bacon side by side on the board, put a tiny piece of sage on top and cover with a piece of chicken. Season the chicken well and add some lemon zest. Cut the cheese into 8 fingers and place one on the piece of chicken. Roll up the bacon and chicken and secure with wooden toothpicks or thread. Continue rolling the rest of the bacon and chicken until you have 8 rolls.

In a heavy pan, brown the rolls in the butter, turning frequently, for about 10 minutes until the chicken appears cooked and the cheese is beginning to melt. Transfer the rolls to a hot dish and remove the toothpicks. Add the wine, vermouth or stock to the pan, scraping up all the sediment, and bubble a few moments to reduce. Add the cream and bubble again 2 to 3 minutes. Taste and adjust the seasoning. Pour a little sauce onto each plate and arrange the rolls on top.

Garnish with lemon wedges and a few sage leaves. Serve with a crisp salad or a green vegetable.
Serves 4

SALAD OF LAMB'S LETTUCE AND DANDELION LEAF WITH BLUE CHEESE

Dandelions are thought to have great curative powers: whether this is true, or not, they make an excellent salad.

8 ounce lamb's lettuce

8 ounce young cultivated dandelion leaves

3 tablespoons wine or cider vinegar

6 bacon slices

1 garlic clove

2 to 3 ounce Cashel blue or other creamy blue cheese

salt and freshly ground black pepper

FOR THE VINAIGRETTE

1 teaspoon French-style mustard

1 tablespoon cider or wine vinegar

4 to 5 tablespoons olive oil

salt and freshly ground black pepper

Rinse the lamb's lettuce; set aside to drain. Rinse the dandelion leaves and trim the stems. Dry well and put them in the salad bowl.

Heat the vinegar. Pour it over the dandelion leaves; toss, and leave for about 15 minutes; this helps to soften them. Pour off any surplus vinegar.

Meanwhile, make the vinaigrette by mixing the mustard, vinegar, and salt and pepper together well. Whisk in the oil until smooth.

Fry the bacon in its own fat, with the garlic, until crisp. Remove the garlic and pour the bacon and pan juices over the dandelions. Add the lamb's lettuce to the bowl and toss well with a little vinaigrette. Season to taste. Crumble the cheese on top. Serve while the bacon is still warm. For a first course, arrange the salad on individual plates.

Serves 6

FRICASSEE OF PORK

1 large onion, chopped

2 tablespoons butter

1 tablespoon oil

4 cups button mushrooms

2 pounds boneless pork, cubed

1 tablespoon all-purpose flour

2 teaspoons ground cumin

²/₃ cup dry white wine or stock

1¹/₄ cups whipping cream

2 celery sticks, thinly sliced

salt and freshly ground black pepper

Preheat the oven to 300°F. Soften the onion in half the butter and oil, then transfer to a baking dish. Add the mushrooms to the pan and cook for a few minutes until lightly browned. Pour, with any juice, into the baking dish. Toss the cubed pork in the flour and cumin and brown in the pan with the remaining oil and butter. Add to the dish. Sprinkle any remaining flour into the pan and stir for a few moments to cook. Add the wine or stock, scraping up all the sediment thoroughly. Stir in the cream, check and adjust the seasoning, and stir well. Pour over the pork mixture. Stir in the sliced celery, cover with a lid or foil and cook until the pork is tender, 45 to 60 minutes. Serve with creamy mashed potatoes or rice.

Serves 6

Lazy beds in Ventry on the Dingle Peninsula

SPRING LAMB CHOPS IN PASTRY

*Easter is the time of renewal and the lamb symbolizes the return of
life in many cultures. Roast baby lamb is traditionally served
for Easter Sunday lunch and nothing is more delicious, especially
when it is moist and tender and delicately pink. As a change from leg
of lamb, try this rack of lamb in pastry, a great party
dish and very easy to carve—simply cut down between the rib bones.
You will need two chops per person, possibly three if they are very
tiny. This sauce is the invariable sauce for lamb in Ireland and
it is very much an eighteenth-century concept; the vinegar was
thought to counteract the fattiness of the meat.*

1 rack of lamb (about 8 rib
  chops; half a hotel rack)
4 tablespoons butter
1 pound thawed commercial
  puff pastry
4 shallots, finely chopped
3 cups finely chopped
  mushrooms
³/₄ cup finely chopped dried
  apricots
chopped fresh mint or
  oregano
1 egg, beaten, to glaze
grated lemon zest and juice
salt and freshly ground
  black pepper

FOR THE MINT SAUCE
1 to 2 tablespoons chopped
  fresh mint
1 to 2 tablespoons sugar,
  or to taste
1 to 2 tablespoons cider or
  white wine vinegar
3 to 4 tablespoons water

Preheat the oven to 425°F. Rub
the lamb with half the butter and
season well. Roast the meat for 8
to 10 minutes. Leave to cool
completely. Reduce the oven

temperature to 350°F.

Gently cook the shallots,
mushrooms, apricots, and mint or
oregano in the remaining butter
until the juices have thickened.
Season this well with lemon zest,
a little lemon juice and plenty of
black pepper. Press the stuffing
between the cutlets. Roll out the
pastry into a sheet large enough
to enclose the rack and fold
around the meat, allowing the
bones to protrude. Cover the
ends of the bones with foil to
prevent them from burning.

Decorate with pastry trimmings.
Brush over the pastry with the
beaten egg. Bake until the pastry is
browned, 25 to 30 minutes.
Serve with mint sauce.

To make the sauce, bring all the
ingredients to a boil; remove from
the heat, stirring to dissolve the
sugar. Leave to cool. (More or less
mint can be used and apple jelly
can be used instead of the sugar.)
Serves 4

CORNED BEEF AND CABBAGE

"Corned" beef, an old word for pickled beef, can be prepared at home using the method for Spiced Beef (see page 118), leaving out the spices.

3 to 4 pounds beef brisket
2 carrots
2 celery sticks
1 onion
1 tablespoon brown sugar
1 tablespoon mustard powder
2 to 3 cloves
1 green or savoy cabbage

Prepare the beef as for Spiced Beef (see page 118) and leave to pickle for 10 days. If you are buying already pickled beef, soak the meat for several hours in cold water.

Put the vegetables and flavorings, except the cabbage, into a large saucepan with the meat. Cover with cold water and bring to a boil very slowly. Simmer gently about 2 hours (20 minutes per pound). When the meat is tender, turn off the heat and leave the meat in the water for 30 minutes, while you prepare the cabbage.

Wash and quarter the cabbage. Pour a ladleful of the cooking water from the meat and enough boiling water to fill a saucepan to half the depth of the cabbage. Add the cabbage and boil hard, without a lid, until it is just tender. Slice the beef and arrange on a deep dish with the cabbage around it.

The traditional method is to put the cabbage into the pot with the meat for the last 15 minutes cooking time, but I feel the lean meat benefits from a resting period and the cabbage is less greasy when cooked on its own. Serve with mustard and plain boiled potatoes.

Serves 6 to 8

IRISH STEW

There is much argument concerning the authentic Irish stew, but for most of us, I suspect, the "authentic" dish is the one made in our own families. The pure tradition uses only mutton, potatoes, onion, and seasoning, and this, I think, is generally agreed to be the thing. Some contemporary recipes include carrots, and even celery, so you can make your own choice.

1 pound onions
2¹/₂ pounds potatoes
2 pounds neck of lamb chops
2 tablespoons butter
2 carrots, chopped
2 celery sticks, chopped
1 large fresh thyme sprig
2 cups water or lamb stock
white pepper and salt

Chop the onions coarsely. Peel and slice the potatoes thickly. Season the chops well. Put the butter in the bottom of a heavy saucepan and then layer the meat and vegetables, finishing with a layer of potatoes. Bury the thyme in the middle. Pour in the stock or water. Cover the pan tightly with foil and a lid. Bring to a boil. Immediately lower the heat and cook gently over the lowest possible heat for about 1¹/₂ hours. The meat and vegetables should cook in their juices with very little liquid left at the end, so watch for burning. It may be necessary to add more liquid.

Serves 6

Ironmongers, Bunratty Folk Park, Co. Clare

SPRING
desserts

IRISH CURD TART

The ancient poetry of Gaelic Ireland has many images of feasting on rich curds, and sweet milk-foods are still enjoyed today.

2 cups cottage cheese

juice and grated zest of
  1 lemon

2 tablespoons sugar, plus a
  little extra

$^1/_2$ cup blanched almonds,
  very finely ground

4 eggs

2 tablespoons raisins

grated nutmeg

FOR THE CRUST

6 tablespoons butter

1 cup all-purpose flour

1 tablespoon sugar

1 egg yolk, beaten

1 to 2 tablespoons very cold
  water

Make the pastry dough in the usual way, cutting the butter into the flour and sugar and moistening with the egg yolk and 1 or 2 tablespoons water, as required. Roll out to fit a greased 8-inch tart pan with a removable bottom. Chill at least 30 minutes.

Preheat the oven to 350°F. Blend or strain the cottage cheese, lemon zest, sugar, and ground almonds. Sharpen to taste, by adding a little lemon juice. Beat the eggs together. Fold the eggs and the raisins into the cheese mixture. Pour into the prepared pastry shell and sprinkle a little sugar and grated nutmeg over the top. Bake 30 to 40 minutes until golden brown; the mixture will gently subside as it cools.

Serve warm or cold. A little whipped cream is good with it, if it's to be served warm.

The raisins can be soaked in a spoonful of whiskey for a few hours first, to plump them up and add a little extra flavor.

Serves 6

Tim Healy Pass, Co. Cork

SIMNEL CAKE

¹/₂ cup (1 stick) butter, softened

6 tablespoons brown sugar

2 tablespoons corn syrup

4 large eggs

1²/₃ cups self-rising flour

1 teaspoon each ground cinnamon, grated nutmeg, and ground ginger

2 cups mixed dried fruit

4 ounces chopped candied citrus peel

1 tablespoon apricot jam, warmed

FOR THE MARZIPAN

1 pound blanched almonds, finely ground

1 cup plus 2 tablespoons superfine sugar

2 cups confectioners' sugar

2 eggs

1¹/₃ tablespoons lemon juice

1 teaspoon almond extract

To make the marzipan, sift the almonds with the sugars. Beat the eggs, lemon juice, and extract together. Stir into the almond mixture, kneading well until a smooth paste forms. Break off eleven walnut-size pieces and roll into balls; set aside (these are said to represent the 12 apostles of Jesus, minus Judas). Divide the remaining piece in half and roll into 2 circles that will fit the cake pan.

Preheat the oven to 325°F. Grease and line a 8-inch x 3-inch-deep cake pan. To make the cake, cream the butter, sugar, and syrup together. Add the eggs, beating well after each addition. Sift the flour and spices together and fold into the batter thoroughly. Fold in the fruit and citrus peel.

Place half the batter in the prepared pan and cover with a layer of marzipan. Put the remaining batter on top. Bake for 1 hour, then cover with a piece of foil, reduce the heat to 300°F and cook for 30 minutes longer. Test with a skewer, but do not push it down into the marzipan layer. The skewer should come out clean. When baked, transfer to a wire rack. Remove from the pan and leave to cool.

When the cake is firm, after about 30 minutes, spread the apricot jam on top and press the second marzipan circle on top, pinching the edge decoratively. Put the cake under a preheated broiler, not too close to the heat, for a few moments to toast the top; watch carefully as it burns quickly. Dampen the marzipan balls and press them around the top of the cake. Lower the broiler rack and return the cake to the broiler to brown the balls.

A yellow ribbon can be tied around the cake for a festive appearance.

ORANGE CREAMS

Seville oranges, both zest and pith, were used to make these delicious creams in the past, when oranges were a seasonal commodity. One Seville orange, with its strong flavor, should be sufficient.

2 oranges
4 egg yolks
2 egg whites
1¹/₄ cups whipping cream and
  whole milk mixed
about 2 tablespoons sugar
1 tablespoon brandy, rum, or
  orange liqueur
whipped cream, to serve

Choose unwaxed oranges, if possible. Scrub the skins well. Using a potato peeler, peel the zest off, not too thinly (a little pith will give more flavor). Squeeze the juice. Put the orange zest, with the juice and a little extra water into a small saucepan and simmer very slowly until the zest is soft. This takes a surprisingly long time, about 45 minutes, and you will probably need to add a few spoonfuls of water from time to time. When the zest is soft, boil the liquid to evaporate, being careful the zest doesn't burn.

Preheat the oven to 300°F. Purée the zest in a mini processor or with a mortar and pestle. Add the eggs, cream and milk, sugar to taste, and the brandy, rum, or liqueur. Pour into 4 buttered ramekins. A strip of peel or a small, skinned orange section can be gently laid on top of each. Set the ramekins in water in a roasting pan. Bake for about 45 minutes until set when tested with a knife. Serve cold, in the ramekins, with a spoonful of whipped cream on top.

Serves 4

CRÊPES

These are traditionally eaten on Shrove Tuesday, the day before Lent begins. Shrove Tuesday crêpes, or pancakes as they are called in Ireland, are served in the simplest manner, with sugar, lemon juice, and butter, and it is hard to improve on this. However, for a simple and delicious dessert, fill them with Cinnamon Custard (see page 37).

1¹/₂ cups all-purpose flour
1 tablespoon superfine sugar
pinch of ground ginger or
  grated nutmeg
2 eggs, beaten
4 tablespoons butter, melted
2¹/₂ cups milk
oil and melted butter for
  frying

Mix the dry ingredients together. Add the eggs, butter, and milk and beat thoroughly. Leave for at least an hour for the flour to expand.

Heat a heavy 7-inch skillet until hot. Add 1 teaspoon each of oil and butter. Swirl around the pan and pour the surplus into a little dish. Pour a small ladleful of batter into the pan and swirl around, to form a thin skin. Cook until golden brown, then turn with a metal spatula and cook for a few moments longer. (The first couple of crêpes invariably break up or stick.) Dip a pastry brush in oil and melted butter and brush the pan again before cooking each crêpe. Stack, with wax paper between each crêpe. They can be reheated in the oven or microwave.

Serves 4

The Skelligs from Puffin Island

CHOCOLATE CAKE WITH MOCCA FILLING

This delicious chocolate cake is suitable either for a luxurious afternoon tea or a dinner-party dessert to celebrate St. Valentine's Day.

FOR THE CAKE

1¹/₂ cups all-purpose flour

³/₄ cup unsweetened cocoa powder

4 large eggs, separated

5 tablespoons sunflower oil

1 cup plus 2 tablespoons sugar

FOR THE FILLING

6 tablespoons butter, softened

1 cup confectioners' sugar, sifted

2 teaspoons instant coffee, dissolved in 1 tablespoon hot water

1 tablespoon rum

TO DECORATE

2 cups whipping cream

1 tablespoon sugar

6 ounce good-quality bitter-sweet chocolate

Preheat the oven to 375°F. Grease and line a deep 8-inch cake pan.

Sift the flour and cocoa together. Beat the egg yolks, oil, and sugar together until pale and creamy. Fold in the flour and cocoa. Beat the egg whites until they form soft peaks and fold carefully into the flour mixture. Pour into the prepared pan, making a depression in the middle. Bake about 45 minutes. Test the cake with a skewer; if it comes out clean, the cake is baked.

Cool the cake in the pan for 10 minutes before turning it onto a cake rack. When cold, slice the cake in half horizontally.

To make the filling, beat the butter with the confectioners' sugar until creamy. Beat in the coffee solution and rum. Spread lavishly on the bottom layer. Assemble the cake; any surplus filling can be spread on the top of the cake.

Whip the cream with the sugar until soft. Reserving some for decoration, cover the entire cake. Using a potato peeler, pare some large flakes of chocolate for the top of the cake; then grate the remainder. Cover the sides of the cake with the grated chocolate using a metal spatula. Pipe the reserved cream around the top and scatter the chocolate flakes in the middle.

Serves 8

Hag's Glen, McGillicuddy's Reeks, Co. Kerry

CINNAMON CUSTARD

This is an ideal filling for crêpes (see page 35), and it also makes a wonderful filling for a sponge cake.

4 egg yolks
¹/₂ cup sugar
¹/₃ cup cornstarch
2¹/₂ cups milk
1 teaspoon grated lemon zest
¹/₂ cinnamon stick
1 vanilla bean

Mix the egg yolks with the sugar and cornstarch.

Bring the milk to a boil slowly, with the cinnamon stick and vanilla bean. Remove from the heat and leave to infuse for 15 minutes.

Remove the cinnamon and vanilla. Return the milk to a boil. Pour onto the egg mixture, stirring rapidly. Return the mixture to the saucepan, over low heat, and stir continually until the custard thickens slightly; do not let it boil or the eggs will scramble. Pour into a shallow bowl and leave to cool.

To serve, fill the crêpes with a few spoonfuls of the custard and sprinkle with a few drops of brandy if you wish. Reheat in a 350°F oven for 15 minutes.

Serves 4

SPRING
baking

RHUBARB CREAM WITH GINGER SNAPS

Creams such as this are found in family recipe books of the eighteenth century, and are the forerunners of the fruit "fools" of today. Ginger cookies contrast well with the creamy rhubarb.

1¹/₂ **pounds rhubarb, washed and trimmed**
4 eggs
¹/₄ **cup sugar**
¹/₂ **cup whipping cream**
1 tablespoon grated lemon zest
2 tablespoons light brown sugar

TO GARNISH
strawberries, sliced if large
fresh lemon balm or mint leaves

Preheat the oven to 325°F. Chop the rhubarb and cook gently, without water until the juice runs and the rhubarb is tender; the microwave is ideal for this. Pour off any excess juice and beat the rhubarb to a purée with a fork.

Beat the eggs with the sugar in a small bowl. Bring the cream to a boil and pour onto the eggs, stirring well. Pour the egg mixture into the rhubarb, add the lemon zest, and stir well. Put the mixture into a 5-cup baking dish. Sprinkle the top with the brown sugar. Stand this in another larger dish filled with water. Bake for about 45 minutes until set around the edge. Remove from the oven and chill.

The cream can be served from the dish or put in glasses and garnished with strawberries and mint or lemon balm leaves.
Serves 4 to 5

GINGER SNAPS
1¹/₂ **cups self-rising flour**
¹/₄ **teaspoon salt**
1 teaspoon ground ginger, or to taste
¹/₂ **cup butter, softened**
scant ¹/₂ **cup light brown sugar**
3 to 4 tablespoons milk

Preheat the oven to 325°F. Sift the flour, salt, and ginger together. Cream the butter and sugar. Fold in the flour and mix to a pliable dough, adding milk as required. Break off walnut-size pieces of dough and roll into balls. Place these on parchment-lined baking trays and press out slightly with the back of a fork dipped in flour. Space out because they will spread. Bake 10 to 12 minutes.

Transfer to a wire rack with a metal spatula; these will keep well in an airtight container.
Makes about 30

Blasket Island, Co. Kerry

HOT-CROSS BUNS

*Hot-cross buns are synonymous with Easter, although, in fact,
they are now thought to predate Christianity.
Whatever their origins, they are delicious, especially toasted with
plenty of butter. They are incomparably better home-made and,
with quick-rising yeast, very easy to make.*

4¹/₂ cups all-purpose flour
1 envelop quick-rising active
  dry yeast
2 teaspoons sugar
1 teaspoon salt
1 tablespoon apple-pie spice,
  or to taste
4 tablespoons butter
1¹/₄ cups milk, warm
1 large egg, beaten
1 cup mixed dried fruit
¹/₂ cup chopped candied
  citrus peel
¹/₂ cup sugar and 1¹/₄ cups
  water, boiled together to
  form a syrup

Mix the flour, yeast, sugar, salt, and
spice together. Melt the butter in
the warm milk and add the
beaten egg.

Make a well in the flour and pour
in the liquid, drawing in the flour
from the sides and kneading well
until a pliable dough forms; this can
be done in a food processor.
Knead in the fruit and citrus peel.
Cover the dough with plastic
wrap and leave to rise until
doubled in bulk.

Punch down the dough and
knead again for a few moments.
Divide into 12 to 14 pieces and
shape into balls. Arrange the balls
on greased baking trays and leave
them to rise for 20 to 30 minutes
longer. Preheat the oven to 375°F.

Mix 2 tablespoons flour and
1 tablespoon water together. Trail
a cross on the top of each bun
with the mixture. Bake for about
20 minutes; they will sound hollow
when tapped underneath.

Using a pastry brush, paint the
buns with the syrup and return to
the oven for 5 minutes to set.
Cool on a wire rack.

WHOLE-WHEAT
SCONES

¹/₂ teaspoon salt
1 tablespoon baking powder
1 cup plus 2 tablespoons all-
  purpose flour
2²/₃ cups stone-ground whole-
  wheat flour
¹/₄ cup brown sugar
6 tablespoons butter, diced
2 eggs
1 cup milk

Preheat the oven to 425°F. Sift the
salt and baking powder with the
white flour. Stir into the whole-
wheat flour. Stir in the sugar and
rub in the butter with your fingers.
Beat the eggs and milk together.
Reserve about 1 tablespoon, and
fold the rest quickly and lightly into
the flour. Add a little more milk, if
necessary, to form a relaxed dough.
Roll out on a lightly floured surface
to 1 inch thick. Cut into circles or
squares. Brush the tops with the
reserved milk and egg mixture.

Bake for about 20 minutes, or
until there is a hollow sound when
the scones are tapped underneath.
Cool on a wire rack.

Country chickens. Overleaf: Coumhoola Valley, Co. Cork

SUMMER

MAY, I think is the most exciting
month in the garden. Suddenly everything
is coming into bloom and, for the cook,
early herbs are abundant.

Sorrel, for wonderful sauces, is ready and waiting for the salmon to become plentiful. In June, thoughts turn to outdoor eating, for many of us one of life's great pleasures though, given the variable Irish climate, picnics in the country or seaside often turn out to be, to quote Dr. Johnson on another subject, "a triumph of hope over experience." All serious picnickers are undeterred by this and indeed some of my happiest recollections involve eating in a downpour, the taste of rain in the wine.

The west of Ireland is the place to be on Midsummer's Night, where the sunset lingers until midnight, and driving through the countryside at night on St. John's Eve, June 23, bonfires can still be seen on the hills, echoes of a ritual older than Christianity.

Ritual brings the summer to a close with the feast of *Lúnasa*, the last Sunday of July, when the custom of picking *fraughauns* (bilberries) still lingers, and was, in fact, the occasion of one of my most memorable rained-out picnics. Perhaps our levity had displeased Crom Dubh, the ancient god of darkness whose feast day this is, and who was said to place his curse on *fraughans* picked after the first of August.

SUMMER
appetizers

POTTED SALMON

This eighteenth-century Irish recipe uses ginger, mace, lemon zest, and bay leaves. There are no exact measurements. The spices can be adjusted to taste and the quantity of fish available, but the initial salting should be generous. This is delicious with toast as a first course or as part of a buffet. The salmon can be potted in individual ramekins, if you prefer.

1 pound salmon
2 tablespoons sea salt
1 teaspoon ground mace
grated zest of 1 lemon
1 bay leaf
pinch of ground ginger
¹/₂ cup (1 stick) butter,
  clarified (see below)

Preheat the oven to 300°F. Skin and remove the bones from the fish and then cut it into pieces. Rub all the surfaces well with salt and leave for 3 hours.

Scrape the salt from the fish, wipe with paper towels but don't wash it. Pack the fish into a baking dish with the mace, lemon zest, and the bay leaf. Cover with foil. Bake for about 30 minutes, or until the fish is cooked through and the flesh flakes easily.

Pour off the juices and remove the bay leaf. Fill the dish up with clarified butter, covering the fish completely. Keep for a day or two before using. To keep for a longer period, up to 10 days, fill the butter up to the depth of ¹/₂ inch over the top of the fish. Keep in the refrigerator.

Note: to clarify butter, melt the butter slowly and let it stand until the sediment falls to the bottom. Carefully pour the clear butter over the fish, leaving the sediment behind.

Serves 6

Dunquaire Castle, Galway Bay
Previous page: Croagh Mharainn, Co. Kerry

CRAB SOUP WITH SAFFRON

4 to 5 saffron strands
6 large scallions, finely
  chopped
1 garlic clove
2 teaspoons fresh marjoram
2 tablespoons butter
3³/₄ cups fish or light
  chicken stock
1 tablespoon long-grain rice
1 tablespoon grated lemon
  zest
12 ounces cooked crabmeat
²/₃ cup whipping cream
salt and freshly ground black
  pepper
1 tablespoon chopped fresh
  parsley, to garnish

Soak the saffron in a little water for 30 minutes. Cook the scallions, garlic, and marjoram in the butter until soft. Add the stock, rice, lemon zest, and saffron, with its water, and simmer until the rice is soft. Add the crab and the cream and season well. Bring back to a boil and simmer 2 to 3 minutes. Serve garnished with the parsley.

Serves 6

SCOTCH EGGS

*In spite of its name, this simple combination of eggs and pork has a long history
in Ireland, and, although somewhat out of fashion, they are still popular for picnics and parties and summer
hors d'oeuvre. A simple mustard mayonnaise makes a good sauce. Scotch eggs also make a very
good lunch, served with buttery creamed potatoes.*

4 large eggs
7 ounce boneless pork, very
  finely ground, or good
  sausage meat
3 scallions, finely
  chopped
2 tablespoons butter
1 tablespoon cornstarch
1 tablespoon Worcestershire
  sauce or soy sauce
1 tablespoon lemon juice
salt and freshly ground black
  pepper
oil for deep-frying

**FOR THE MUSTARD
MAYONNAISE**
2 egg yolks, at room
  temperature
1 tablespoon mild French-
  style mustard
1¹/₄ cups olive oil
about 1 tablespoon horseradish
  cream
salt

Boil the eggs for 10 minutes in plenty of water. Sauté the scallions in the butter until soft; leave to cool. Mix the pork, scallions, cornstarch, and Worcestershire or soy sauce, lemon juice, and salt and pepper together to make a paste. Shell the eggs and dry them carefully.

Divide the pork into 4 portions and, with floured hands, shape around each egg, encasing it completely. Deep-fry the eggs in sufficient oil to cover them, turning frequently to prevent them from splitting, for 6 to 8 minutes. Drain on paper towels.

For an appetizer or for a buffet, slice the eggs lengthwise and arrange on crisp lettuce. For a picnic leave them whole.

To make the mustard mayonnaise, mix the egg yolks with the mustard. Gradually beat in the oil, drop by drop at first, and then in a thin stream as it begins to emulsify. Use a wooden spoon and beat continuously, or use an electric beater on medium speed. Season well with a pinch of salt and add creamed horseradish, to taste. If the mayonnaise separates, put another egg yolk in a clean bowl and add the mixture, drop by drop, as before.

Serves 4

Hill path, Co. Kerry

LOVAGE SOUP

Lovage, once to be found in every Irish garden, has celery-like leaves that make interesting soups and salads. Celery leaves can be prepared in the same way.

2 tablespoons butter
1 onion, finely chopped
1 garlic clove, finely chopped
2 to 3 large handfuls young
  lovage or celery leaves
1 tablespoon lemon juice
1 tablespoon all-purpose flour
2¹/₂ cups chicken stock, hot
2¹/₂ cups milk
salt and freshly ground
  black pepper
fresh lovage leaves, to garnish
4 tablespoons croutons

Melt the butter in a large saucepan. Add the onion and garlic and cook until soft. Add the chopped lovage and lemon juice and cook until the leaves soften a little. Sprinkle in the flour and continue stirring until the flour is cooked and the sauce is smooth. Gradually stir in half the hot stock, stirring well, until the flour has cooked. Purée in a food processor or blender.

Return to the pan, add the rest of the stock and the milk, and bring back to a boil. Season with plenty of black pepper and salt to taste. Just before serving, garnish with fresh lovage leaves and croutons.

Note: to make croutons, remove the crusts from 3 slices of white bread, and cut the bread into cubes. Fry in a little oil until brown. Drain on paper towels.

Serves 6

Ben Bulben, Co. Sligo

PEA POD SOUP

*The pods of baby peas, so juicy
and sweet, make very good
soup, with an intense pea taste.
Sugar-snap peas give almost
the same flavor.*

8 ounce (1¹/₂ cups) sugar-
  snap peas
1 onion, finely chopped
2 tablespoons butter
2 tablespoons flour
3 cups chicken or vegetable
  stock, hot
fresh mint or summer savory,
  roughly chopped
¹/₂ teaspoon sugar
1 tablespoon chopped parsley
salt and freshly ground
  black pepper
3 to 4 tablespoons whipping
  cream
chopped fresh mint, to
  garnish

Rinse the peas. Place them in a
saucepan, just barely cover with
water and simmer until they are
tender, about 15 minutes. Strain
the peas and keep the water.

Cook the onion in the butter,
until soft. Stir in the flour and stir
until cooked, 2 to 3 minutes.
Gradually add half the hot stock,
stirring until the sauce thickens.
Add the mint or savory. Purée this
mixture, with the peas, in a
blender or food processor until
smooth. Return to the saucepan.

Stir in the remainder of the
stock, the sugar, parsley, and salt
and pepper. Check the seasoning
and bring to a boil for 2 to 3
minutes. A little of the pea water
can be added, for a thinner soup.
Serve in small bowls, with a little
cream in each. Garnish with mint.
Serves 4

SMOKED SALMON PÂTÉ

12 ounces smoked salmon
³/₄ cup crème fraîche or sour cream
grated zest and juice of ¹/₂ lemon
fresh dill sprigs
6 tablespoons butter, melted
¹/₂ cup heavy cream

TO DECORATE
small fresh dill sprigs
gherkins

Skin and chop the salmon, removing any bones. Put it in a food processor with the crème fraîche or sour cream, lemon zest and juice, a few sprigs of dill, and 4 tablespoons of the melted butter. Purée to a smooth paste. Transfer to a bowl and gradually beat in the cream.

Rub 6 ramekins with oil and pack the pâté into them. Brush the tops with the remaining butter, cover and chill.

To serve, decorate with dill and gherkins. Serve with toast.
Serves 6

White Bull Head, West Cork

CHICKEN, ORANGE, AND ARUGULA SALAD WITH WALNUT SAUCE

Large boneless, skinless chicken breasts, weighing about 1 pound in total
1¹/₄ cups chicken stock
18 to 20 arugula leaves
2 large sweet oranges
salt

FOR THE SAUCE
³/₄ cup walnut halves
1 tablespoon cider or sherry vinegar
3 tablespoons walnut or olive oil
2 teaspoons sugar
1 garlic clove
reserved stock

Place the chicken in a saucepan and barely cover with the stock. Add water, if necessary. Add a pinch of salt and poach gently until cooked but still juicy, 10 to 15 minutes. Strain the stock and reserve for the sauce. Shred the chicken by pulling it apart with 2 forks, lengthwise, with the grain of the meat.

Rinse and dry the arugula leaves and put in the refrigerator to crisp.

To make the sauce, toast the walnuts in a dry pan until crisp and very slightly brown. Put them in a blender with the other sauce ingredients and half the reserved stock. Grind to a smooth paste. Adjust to taste, adding more vinegar or sugar as required. Dilute to a thin purée with some of the remaining stock; reserve 2 tablespoons of sauce to finish.

Peel the oranges with a sharp knife and then slice down between the membranes, separating the flesh from the dividing membrane; allow 2 or 3 slices per person. (All of this can be prepared ahead of time, or the day before.)

To serve, pour a small pool of sauce on each plate and arrange the chicken, orange, and arugula on each. Thin the remaining 2 tablespoons of sauce with stock or oil and drizzle over the top.
Serves 6

SUMMER
main courses

CHICKEN AND HAM PASTIES

A pastie is a meat and vegetable mixture enclosed in pastry. The combination of chicken and ham is perennially popular in Ireland. These old-fashioned pasties make an excellent lunch or simple dinner, and are indispensable picnic fare. Serve with new potatoes and a salad.

1¹/₂ cups finely chopped
  cooked chicken
1¹/₂ cups finely chopped ham
2 small leeks, finely chopped
1¹/₄ cups sliced mushrooms
4 tablespoons butter
1 tablespoon all-purpose flour
1¹/₄ cups milk, hot
¹/₂ teaspoon coriander seeds
1 teaspoon poppy seeds
salt and freshly ground
  black pepper

FOR THE PASTRY
2²/₃ cups all-purpose flour
1 cup (2 sticks) butter, diced
1 small egg, beaten, to glaze
salt, pinch

Make the pastry dough in the usual way by rubbing the butter into the flour and salt and moistening with 2 to 4 tablespoons of cold water. Roll out into four 6-inch circles. Chill at least 30 minutes.

Sauté the leeks with the mushrooms in 2 tablespoons of the butter; set aside.

Melt the remaining butter in a saucepan. Stir in the flour and heat gently for 2 minutes. Gradually add the hot milk, stirring continuously until the sauce thickens. Season well. Add the coriander seeds and the leek mixture and its juices. Cool. Preheat the oven to 375°F.

Fold the finely chopped meats into the sauce. When it is cool, divide between the dough circles. Dampen the edges and draw the 2 sides together, pinching well to seal. Place, seam-side down, on a greased cookie sheet. Brush with beaten egg and sprinkle with poppy seeds. Bake until the pastry is golden, 20 to 25 minutes. Serve hot or cold.

Serves 4

MACKEREL WITH GOOSEBERRY SAUCE

This is another combination that has its origins in the past, when fruit sauces with fish or meat were considered good for the digestion. Applesauce with pork is another example.
The elderflowers give a delicate muscatel flavor, and were often added to apple and gooseberry tarts. If elderflowers are unavailable, try substituting nasturtium or other mild edible flower heads. The sauce can be hot or cold, as you prefer, and is equally good with pork.

6 mackerel, dressed
1 pound gooseberries
1 to 2 heads elderflowers
2 to 3 tablespoons water
sugar, to taste
2 tablespoons all-purpose
  flour
1 egg, beaten
3 tablespoons steel-cut oats
butter and oil for frying
salt and freshly ground
  black pepper

Cook the gooseberries and elderflowers with the water until soft. Remove the elderflowers and sweeten to taste. Push through a strainer; set aside.

Rinse and dry the mackerel, removing heads if preferred. Season the insides and flour well. Dip the mackerel in the beaten egg and roll in the oats. Melt 1 tablespoon each of butter and oil in a large skillet. Add the mackerel and fry over low heat until the flesh is opaque. Drain on paper towels. Serve with the gooseberry sauce and creamy mashed potatoes, to which you have added finely chopped scallions and lots of black pepper.

Serves 6

Slea Head, Co. Kerry

BAKED SALMON WITH A
HERB CRUST

Although excellent farmed salmon is available all year round, the creamy, curdy texture of wild salmon in May is perfection.

1-inch cube fresh gingerroot
6 canned anchovy fillets,
   drained
¹/₂ cup (1 stick) butter
3 tablespoons finely chopped
   scallions
3 tablespoons finely chopped
   fresh parsley
grated zest of 1 lemon
3 to 5 pounds salmon, in 2
   fillets, skinned
³/₄ cup bread crumbs, made
   from day-old bread

FOR THE SAUCE
3 egg yolks
1¹/₄ cups whipping cream
5 to 6 sorrel leaves, ribs
   removed and leaves chopped
grated zest of 1 lemon
1 tablespoon chopped fresh
   cilantro or parsley
salt and freshly ground
   black pepper

Preheat the oven to 325°F. Mash the ginger to a paste with the anchovies, 6 tablespoons of the butter, scallions, parsley, and half the grated zest. Butter a sheet of baking parchment which will fit the salmon and line a baking tray. Lay one fillet of salmon on the paper and spread with half the herb butter. Lay the other fillet on top, reversing the wide end over the narrow end of the bottom fillet. Spread the remaining herb butter over the top.

Cover the salmon with the bread crumbs, patting them down lightly. Season well and dot with the remaining butter. Bake for 12 minutes per pound for smaller fish; a 6 to 7 pound fish will not require more than an hour.

When baked through, use the baking paper to lift the fish onto a heated serving dish. Retain the juices for the sauce.

To make the sauce, season the egg yolks and beat together. Bring the cream to a boil with the sorrel leaves and lemon zest. Cook to reduce for a few moments. Pour onto the yolks, stirring well and then return to the pan. Over low heat, cook, stirring continuously and without allowing the sauce to boil, until it thickens slightly. Pour the strained fish juices into the sauce, add the cilantro or parsley and serve.

Serves 6 as a main course, or 8 to 10 as part of a buffet

SCALLOPS WITH TARRAGON SAUCE

Tender, juicy scallops need very little cooking. Be sure to save the red corals when cleaning them.

³/₄ cup dry white wine
6 tablespoons water
grated zest and juice of ¹/₂ lemon
4 to 5 fresh tarragon leaves or a pinch of dried tarragon
12 scallops, shucked
6 tablespoons whipping cream
1 tablespoon butter
3 egg yolks, beaten
1 tablespoon chopped fresh parsley

Put the wine, water, lemon juice and zest, and tarragon leaves in a saucepan. Boil for 2 to 3 minutes. Add the scallops and their corals and gently poach for about 5 minutes until they are no longer translucent and are firm to the touch. Transfer to a warm place.

Strain the cooking liquid into a small saucepan and boil rapidly to reduce slightly. Add the cream and butter and boil for 2 to 3 minutes. Pour onto the egg yolks, whisking well all the time. Return the mixture to the pan over very low heat and continue to stir until the sauce thickens slightly; do not let it boil. Season well and add the parsley and more tarragon, if desired.

Arrange the scallops on warm plates and pour the sauce over. Creamy mashed potatoes are the classic companion for scallops.

Serves 3 to 4 as a main course, depending on the size of the scallops

Oughterard house front, Co. Galway

HAM IN PASTRY

Hams, and the art of cooking them, are well understood in Ireland and they are always popular for grand occasions. If the ham is to be eaten hot, seasonal vegetables and a well-made parsley sauce are the traditional partners. Rowanberry or cranberry jelly, heated with a glass of port and a little orange juice, also makes an excellent sauce.

6 to 8 pound boneless ham
juniper berries
2 bay leaves
1 large onion, halved
2 to 3 tablespoons brown
   sugar
1 tablespoon mustard powder
2 tablespoons Dijon-style mild
   mustard
2 pounds prepared pastry
   dough or piecrust dough
1 egg, beaten, to glaze

Soak the ham overnight in cold water if it seems to be salty; otherwise 1 to 2 hours will do.

When ready to cook, put the ham in a large saucepan, with a few juniper berries, the bay leaves, and the onion halves. Add the sugar and mustard powder, and cover with cold water. Timing from when the water boils, simmer for 20 minutes per pound; test for tenderness with a skewer before the last 20 minutes, as it may not be necessary. The ham will cook a little more in the oven. When cooked, leave to cool for about 30 minutes in the water, then remove and peel off the skin and some of the fat if there is too much. Leave the ham to cool completely. Preheat the oven to 375°F.

Roll out the dough into a large square that will cover the ham, keeping it quite thick; about ¼ inch. Rub the mustard over the ham, then cover it completely with the dough, trimming the surplus and dampening and sealing the joins. Place on a baking tray, keeping the seams underneath as far as possible.

Brush the beaten egg over. Use the trimmings to make leaves or other decorations, and brush with the egg again. Make a steam vent at the highest point.

Bake for about 20 minutes. Cover the pastry loosely with foil, lower the heat to 325°F and continue baking about 45 minutes longer until the ham is completely heated through.

Serves 10 as a main course, 25 as part of a buffet

Upper Caragh River, Co. Kerry

GELLED TONGUE

Liked and disliked with equal intensity, a pressed beef tongue is an essential ingredient of any Irish cold meat platter, and, although it takes a long time to cook, the preparation is extremely simple. A little port added to the stock results in a richer jelly. Small, trimmed tongues are available from the meat counter of supermarkets and some delicatessens and do not usually require soaking; larger tongues may need soaking overnight.

1 tongue, weighing about 2 pounds
1 each onion, carrot, and celery stick
2 teaspoons black peppercorns
1 orange
glass of port
1 envelope or 4 teaspoons unflavored gelatin

Place the tongue in a large saucepan and cover with cold water. Add the vegetables, peppercorns and a large strip of orange zest. Bring to a boil very slowly and simmer until a skewer will slide in easily; this can take 2 to 4 hours, depending on its size. Remove the tongue from the water when cool enough to handle and peel off the skin and any gristle. Return the tongue to the stock, to keep warm.

Strain off 1½ cups of the cooking liquid and use a little to dissolve the gelatin, according to the package directions. Put the remainder in a small saucepan, with the port and the juice of ½ orange. Boil hard to reduce for 1 to 2 minutes. Remove from the heat and add the dissolved gelatin. Put the warm tongue in a bowl or mold that will just hold it. Pour enough of the port mixture over to cover it when it is pressed down well with a plate or saucer. Put a weight or tin cans on top of the plate and leave overnight. Leave the remaining port mixture to set, to use as the garnish.

To serve, remove any fat from the top. Unmold the tongue and carve in thin slices. Decorate with the chopped port mixture jelly. Spicy Cumberland sauce or horseradish cream can be served with it.

Serves 6 as a main course, 8 to 10 as part of a buffet

RAGOUT OF SCALLOPS AND BACON

8 scallops, shucked
2 tablespoons butter
4 bacon slices
1 onion, chopped
2 to 3 scallions, chopped
3 cups mixed shiitake and
   oyster mushrooms
2 teaspoons all-purpose flour
²/₃ cup dry white wine
²/₃ cup whipping cream
1 tablespoon chopped fresh
   parsley
1 teaspoon chopped fresh dill
   or chervil
1 tablespoon lemon juice
salt and freshly ground black
   pepper

Remove the red corals, and then slice each scallop into 3 pieces horizontally. Sauté them gently with the corals for 1 to 2 minutes in half the butter. Fry the bacon until crisp, then chop finely. Cook the onion and mushrooms in the bacon fat, adding the remaining butter, for 2 to 3 minutes. Sprinkle in the flour, stirring well until the flour is cooked. Stir in the wine and bubble until the sauce thickens, then add the cream, bacon, parsley, dill, and a little lemon juice. Adjust the seasoning and bring back to a boil. Add the scallops and let them heat through, 2 to 3 minutes.

Serves 4

PICKLED HARD-BOILED EGGS

In the not-too-distant past, when Irish pubs were quiet retreats for serious drinking men and "pub grub" hadn't been thought of, large jars of pickled eggs stood on old bar counters, luminescent in the near-silent gloom, the only concession to food.

Hard-boil the eggs by placing them in a large saucepan of cold water. Bring the water to a boil, remove it from the heat, and leave to stand, covered, for 15 minutes. Transfer the eggs to cold running water and peel carefully.

When completely cool, put the eggs in large canning jars, which have plastic-lined lids. Cover them completely with white-wine vinegar. Add a few peppercorns to each jar. (Distilled vinegar can also be used.) Refrigerate for about two weeks before serving.

Kilkenny, a town rich in pubs

PEAS AND LETTUCE

This combination of two summer vegetables is more than 200 years old, and, although its origins are French, it is found in almost every Irish family recipe collection of the past. Nowadays, it need not wait for summer, frozen petits pois make a reasonable substitute for the tender young summer peas and they can be used straight away, without blanching. This vegetable dish is equally delicious eaten with fish or meat.

1 head of butterhead-type lettuce (with a heart), such as Boston or Bibb
4 tablespoons butter
3 to 4 scallions, finely chopped
1 pound frozen petits pois, thawed, or tender young fresh peas, blanched
chopped fresh chervil or summer savory
ground mace or grated nutmeg
salt and freshly ground black pepper

Wash and dry the lettuce. Stack the leaves on top of each other, roll up gently, and cut at 1-inch intervals to make fine strips.

Melt the butter in a saucepan and gently cook the scallions. Add the peas, lettuce, herbs, and flavoring. Cook very gently for about 10 minutes.

Serves 6

The Blasket Islands from Slea Head, Co. Kerry

ROAST BEEF SALAD

*A tenderloin of Irish beef needs little adornment and is at its best
simply prepared. For this summery salad, both beef and sauce
can be prepared well in advance.*

FOR THE SALAD

1½ pounds beef tenderloin,
  in one piece
4 tablespoons olive oil
2 tablespoons red-wine vinegar
2 garlic cloves, crushed
2 teaspoons ground allspice
1 tablespoon Dijon-style
  mustard
2 bunches scallions
olive oil
mixed salad greens, herb
  leaves, cherry tomatoes,
  marigold petals, chive or
  arugula flowers

FOR THE SAUCE

4 tablespoons white-wine
  vinegar
1 teaspoon black peppercorns
2 teaspoons each chopped
  fresh tarragon and parsley,
  mixed
4 tablespoons water
4 egg yolks
¾ cup (1½ sticks) butter,
  softened

Trim the meat of any fat and tie it
at intervals to keep its shape while
cooking. Marinate the meat at
room temperature in the oil,
vinegar, and crushed garlic for 2
to 3 hours.

Preheat the oven to 425°F.
Remove the beef from the
marinade and wipe dry with paper
towels. Mix the allspice and
mustard together and spread over
the meat. Roast the meat for 20
minutes; this will give pink beef.
Cook for 5 to 7 minutes longer if
preferred. Five minutes before the
end of the cooking time, brush the

scallions with more olive oil and
scatter over the meat. Remove
the meat and cool.

To make the sauce, boil the
vinegar, peppercorns, and 1
teaspoon of the herbs with the
water until reduced to 2
tablespoons. Strain into a small
bowl over hot water, or use a
double-boiler, and beat in the egg
yolks. Stir well until the yolks are
warm; then gradually stir in the
softened butter, in walnut-size
lumps, stirring until the sauce
thickens slightly and coats the back
of a spoon. Stir continually, lifting
the saucepan on and off the heat
to prevent it from overheating
and scrambling the eggs. When
the sauce has thickened, pour it
into a blender and whizz for a few
moments, until it becomes slightly
foamy. Add the remaining herbs,
cover and set aside. (If you do not
have a blender, whisk hard with a
wire whisk.) Pour into a sauce
boat or dish to serve.

Arrange the salad greens and
other leaves attractively on a large
serving dish. Untie the beef and
slice very thinly. Arrange in an
overlapping circle and put the
wilted scallions in the middle.
(The beef will lose its color if
sliced too soon.) Garnish with the
tomatoes and whatever herb
flowers are to hand, such as
marigold petals or chive or
arugula flowers. Spoon a little
vinaigrette over the leaves just
before serving.

SUMMER
desserts

STRAWBERRIES IN GELLED WINE

*Eating strawberries with red wine is a very old custom, the acidity of both being
tempered by the liberal use of sugar and spice. Choose a wine you like to drink.
"How I like Claret! When I can get Claret, I must drink it....
If you could make some wine like Claret to drink on summer evenings in an arbour ..."*
John Keats, letter to his brother, 1819

**2 envelopes or 8 teaspoons
    unflavored gelatin**
scant $^1/_2$ cup red-currant jelly
$^1/_2$ cup sugar, or to taste
1 cinnamon stick
2 to 3 tablespoons water
**$2^1/_2$ cups red wine, such as
    from Bordeaux**
2 tablespoons brandy
2 tablespoons lemon juice
12 ounces strawberries
**strawberries and fruits,
    to decorate**

Rinse the strawberries well and hull them. Put 3 to 4 tablespoons of the wine in a bowl and sprinkle the gelatin over it. When the gelatin has softened, stand the bowl in hot water and stir until the gelatin completely dissolves. Keep the mixture warm.

Heat the red-currant jelly, sugar, and cinnamon stick in a saucepan with the water until both sugar and jelly dissolve. Remove the cinnamon and strain into a large bowl. Add the gelatin and stir thoroughly. When cool add the remaining wine, brandy, and lemon juice.

Pour half the mixture and half the strawberries into a dampened 5-cup mold and leave to cool.

Warm the remaining jelly mixture, add the rest of the strawberries and fill up the mold. (If this operation is done all at once, the strawberries will float to the top.) Chill when cool. Unmold when completely set and decorate with fruits, flowers, and leaves.

Have a bowl of whipped cream on hand, for those who like it. One or 2 geranium leaves, infused in the cream for an hour or so, give a subtle flavor.

Serves 6

Garinish Island, Co. Cork

STRAWBERRY-CHOCOLATE ROLL

*Jelly rolls and chocolate rolls are favorite components
of the Irish tea table. This strawberry-filled chocolate roll is rich
enough for an elegant summer dinner party.*

FOR THE CAKE
$^1/_2$ cup all-purpose flour
$^1/_4$ cup unsweetened cocoa
  powder
$^1/_2$ teaspoon baking powder
2 extra-large eggs
$^1/_2$ cup superfine sugar
2 tablespoons hot water
confectioners' sugar, sifted, to
  decorate

FOR THE FILLING
1 cup heavy cream
$^1/_4$ cup superfine sugar
brandy or vanilla extract
1 pound strawberries,
  cleaned and hulled

Preheat the oven to 425°F.
Butter a small (15 x 10 inch) jelly-
roll pan and line with baking
parchment. Cut another piece of
parchment the same size and have
ready a dish towel, wrung out in
hot water.

Sift the flour, cocoa, and baking
powder. Beat the eggs and sugar
together until thick, white, and
creamy. Using a large metal spoon,
fold in the flour, cutting with the
edge of the spoon, and turning,
rather than mixing. Finally, fold in
the hot water. Pour into the pan
and smooth the top with a spatula.
Bake 7 to 10 minutes until the
batter slightly shrinks away from
the sides; if the sponge is
overbaked, it becomes dry.

Put the piece of baking
parchment on the hot dish towel
and sprinkle it with sugar. Turn the
cake out on top. Quickly trim the
edges and peel the baking paper
away. Carefully roll up, with the
fresh paper inside. Leave to cool.

Stiffly whip the cream with a little
sugar and brandy or vanilla extract.
Chop three-quarters of the
strawberries and fold them into
the cream. Carefully unroll the
chocolate roll and remove the
paper. Fill with the strawberry mix,
roll up the cake and dredge with a
little confectioners' sugar. Decorate
with the remaining strawberries.
  Serves 6

Sligo thatch

ROSE PETAL ICE CREAM

Scented roses are one of the great pleasures of summer. To make the most of them when they are at their peak, try this romantic ice cream.

2¹/₂ cups red or pink
  scented rose petals
¹/₂ cup superfine sugar
1¹/₄ cups rosé wine
5 egg yolks
1 vanilla bean or 1 teaspoon
  vanilla extract
1¹/₄ cups milk
1¹/₄ cups heavy cream
1 teaspoon rose water
  (obtainable in Oriental
  grocers)
crystallized rose petals, to
  decorate (see below)

To prepare the rose petals, wipe them clean with damp paper towels. Cut away the hard white stem or heel. Purée them in a blender or food processor, with half the sugar, and the wine.

Beat the eggs and remaining sugar thoroughly. Split the vanilla bean, if using, and add to the milk and cream. Bring to a boil and simmer gently for a few moments to infuse. Remove the bean (add vanilla extract now, if using). Pour the hot mixture onto the eggs and sugar and return to the saucepan, stirring continuously. Heat to just below boiling point; do not let it boil. The custard is ready when you remove the spoon and the mixture on it remains separated when you run your finger through it. Leave to cool.

Stir in the rose purée and rose water. Taste for sweetness. Freeze in the usual way, by stirring and beating the mixture 2 or 3 times during the freezing process. To serve, decorate with crystallized rose petals.

Note: to make crystallized rose petals, prepare the rose petals as for the ice cream. Beat one large egg white until just fluid. Dip each petal into the egg white and then dredge in superfine sugar, covering completely. Spread the petals on a foil-lined baking tray and dry in a very low oven, with the door ajar, for an hour or so until they are crisp. Store in an airtight container, between sheets of waxed paper. Use for cake decoration also.

Serves 4

A Donegal window

CHERRY MOUSSE

1 pound cherries
1 tablespoon each grated
  lemon zest and lemon juice
1 envelope or 4 teaspoons
  unflavored gelatin
4 eggs
¹/₄ cup superfine sugar
²/₃ cup whipping cream
summer fruits or fresh mint
  leaves, to decorate

Poach the cherries in as little water as possible until soft enough to extract the pits. Purée the cherries with 1 to 2 tablespoons of their juice and the lemon zest and juice. Use the remaining juice to dissolve the gelatin according to the directions on the package; leave to cool.

Separate the eggs and put the yolks and sugar in a bowl over hot water. Whisk, over low heat, until thick and creamy. Remove from the heat and whisk from time to time until cool. Thoroughly stir the gelatin into the egg mixture; then beat in the cherry purée. Lightly whip the cream and fold it in. Whisk the egg whites to the soft-peak stage and, when the gelatin mixture is on the point of setting, fold the whites in carefully, amalgamating them thoroughly.

Divide the mousse between 6 ring molds or ramekins and leave to set. Decorate with berries or mint leaves.

Serves 6

SYLLABUB

In the seventeenth century, this was a popular confection of wine, hard cider, or fruit juice to which milk was added by force, often by milking the cow directly into the other ingredients to make froth, or bubbles. Nowadays, it takes only minutes to prepare. In earlier times, syllabub was the traditional covering for trifle, before the use of whipped cream became universal, and macaroons often formed the base.

1¼ cups whipping cream
3 tablespoons sweet white
  wine or sherry
juice of ½ orange
grated zest of ½ lemon
¼ cup superfine sugar

TO DECORATE
summer fruits
Macaroons (see page 103)

Whip all the ingredients together until thick and creamy. Carefully spoon into 4 glasses. Make the syllabub a few hours in advance to let the flavors develop.
  Garnish with berries and serve with macaroons.
  Serves 4

LOGANBERRY AND PLUM JAM

Its fun to make small quantities of different jams with whatever is to hand, and this intensely flavored combination is well worth the half hour it takes. If gooseberries aren't available, use more lemon juice. If loganberries are difficult to find, substitute raspberries or blackberries.

1 pound plums
4 ounce gooseberries
1³/₄ cups plus 2 tablespoons water
1 pound loganberries
4¹/₂ cups superfine sugar
juice of ¹/₂ lemon

Simmer the plums and gooseberries in the water until the plums are soft enough to remove the pits. Cut the plums in pieces, if they are large, and return them to the water.

Add the loganberries, bring back to the boil, and cook for 5 minutes. Remove from the heat, pour in the sugar and lemon juice and stir until completely dissolved. Boil hard for 7 to 10 minutes until a few drops cooled on a chilled saucer wrinkle when pushed with a finger. Pour into hot, sterilized pots and cover.

Fills 5 x ¹/₂-pint jars

Summer cows

Summer

RASPBERRY JAM

*The raspberry season is so
short, but jams and preserves
help to prolong the taste
of summer.*

3 pounds raspberries
3-pound bag superfine sugar
8 ounce red currants or
 2 tablespoons lemon juice

Put the sugar in a baking dish and
warm gently in the oven.

Warm the fruit in a stainless
steel saucepan over very low heat
until the juice begins to flow. Bring
very slowly to a boil and simmer
for 10 minutes. Pour in the warmed
sugar and lemon juice, if using, and
stir until the sugar completely
dissolves. Boil hard until it sets
when tested. Start testing after 8
minutes. Put some saucers to chill
in the freezer and then test by
putting a few drops of the mixture
on a saucer and leaving it to cool;
if the surface of the drop wrinkles
when pushed with a finger, the jam
is ready. Pot in hot, dry, sterilized
jars and seal immediately.

Fills 5 x 12-ounce jars

ROSE PETAL VINEGAR

*Use this delicate vinegar to
flavor summer salads,
or try a few drops on summer
fruits, such as strawberries
and raspberries; it brings out
the flavors.*

The choice of the base vinegar is
important. Use a good-quality
white-wine vinegar, or organic
cider vinegar. Rice vinegar, which
can be bought from Oriental
stores, is particularly delicate in
flavor. Measure equal quantities of
vinegar and scented rose petals—
about 2 large cupfuls of each. Put
them together in a glass or
porcelain container and cover
tightly. They should be left to steep
on a sunny window for at least 3
weeks. If you like a stronger flavor,
strain off the petals and add fresh
ones; then steep a little longer.

Strain into bottles and cork
tightly. Elderflower vinegar can be
made the same way.

Haycocks, Co. Kerry
Overleaf: Killarney, Co. Kerry

FALL

AUGUST is the month when the lazy beds give up their new potatoes; this was once a significant date, but is now unnoticed, when potatoes of all sizes and ages, from all over Europe and, apparently, independent of season, are in the stores.

Oysters, too, are taken from their beds (the superb native oyster even merits its own festival in Galway at this time of year) and will be plentiful and good during the fall and winter, when they'll be consumed in quantity and washed down with Guinness. In the days before tea became the other national beverage, when hard cider and beer were consumed by young and old, apple and pear orchards were abundant in the countryside. Some of these areas still retain their fame: Armagh has given its name to many apple dishes, as has Clonmel, where excellent cider is still made today.

Mushrooms make their appearance in late summer and early fall and their mysterious nature has been a source of fascination from earliest times. The rapidity of growth, the fact they appear to grow at night and are there, waiting, in the early morning, has given rise to a wide folklore and numerous old wives' tales, such as using a silver spoon when cooking mushrooms—it was supposed to turn black if the mushrooms were poisonous. Hallowe'en is the climax of fall and, perhaps, the favorite festival of children. Old traditions live on and apples, studded with coins, and floating in bowls of water, are still bobbed for. Dressing up, wearing masks, and carving pumpkins (it used to be turnips) are as popular as ever. Colcannon is made, slices of brack are scrutinized in hopes of finding a ring and a sweetheart, fortunes are told, and there are bonfires, too.

FALL
appetizers

MUSHROOMS IN PASTRY

There is a charm in mushrooms that is never quite dispelled by familiarity. Use as many kinds as you can find; their different flavors blend together interestingly.

8 ounce spinach

4 to 6 tablespoons butter

1 garlic clove, finely chopped

6¹/₂ cups mixed mushrooms

2 tablespoons mushroom
  ketchup

salt and freshly ground
  black pepper

¹/₂ teaspoon cayenne pepper

12 ounce commercial or
  homemade puff pastry dough

1 egg, beaten

²/₃ cup whipping cream

Preheat the oven to 375°F. Wash and coarsely chop the spinach. Melt a knob of butter in a large skillet. Add the garlic and slowly cook for a few moments. Add the spinach and toss until it is softly wilted. Remove and squeeze any juices back into the pan.

Wipe and trim the mushrooms and chop them coarsely. Add another tablespoon of butter and half the ketchup to the pan and cook the mushrooms until they are reduced but still juicy. Season well with salt, pepper, and cayenne. (If oyster mushrooms are used don't put them in until the last moment.) Remove the mushrooms to cool but leave the juices in the pan.

Roll out the dough into 2 large rectangles, about 9 x 6 inch each. Place one on a greased baking sheet and cover it with the spinach, then pile on the mushrooms, leaving a ¹/₂-inch space around the edges. Dot with butter and then cover with the other rectangle of dough. Press the dampened edges together and make a steam vent in the top. Brush with the beaten egg. Bake until golden, about 40 minutes.

Add the cream, remaining butter, and mushroom ketchup to the juices in the pan and bubble for a few moments, to make a little sauce.

Serves 8

The Paps, Co. Kerry
Previous page: near Bantry, Co. Cork

SMOKED SALMON TARTLETS

These delicate little tartlets, filled with smoked salmon mousse, can be garnished with whatever suits taste and season: anchovies and capers, quail's eggs, or salmon roes.

FOR THE PASTRY
2 cups all-purpose flour
½ teaspoon grated lemon
  zest
1¼ cups butter, chilled and
  diced
1 egg yolk
1 tablespoon very cold water
salt

FOR THE FILLING
8 ounce smoked salmon
1 cup crème fraîche or sour
  cream
2 teaspoons finely chopped
  fresh dill or tarragon
½ teaspoon paprika
2 teaspoons lemon juice
Tabasco or bottled chili sauce
fresh chervil or tarragon
  leaves, to garnish

TO SERVE
oil and balsamic vinegar
mixed salad leaves

To make the pastry dough, sift the flour with a pinch of salt. Stir in the lemon zest and cut in the butter. Moisten with the egg yolk and cold water. Chill for at least half an hour.

Preheat the oven to 375°F. Roll out the dough to fit six 3-inch buttered tartlet pans with removable bottoms. Fill the pans with the dough and prick the bottoms. Line with baking parchment and then fit the pans into each other, putting an empty pan (or foil and dried beans) into the top pan. Bake for 15 minutes. Remove the pans from the oven, separate, and put back for 5 minutes or so, until crisp but not too brown. (These can be made in advance and kept in an airtight container. Don't fill them, however, until shortly before serving, so they remain crisp.)

Put the salmon and crème fraîche or sour cream in a blender or food processor, with the herbs, paprika, lemon juice, and a dash of Tabasco or chili sauce. Process until a stiff purée forms. Add a little more cream, if it's too stiff. Chill until required.

Divide the filling between the pastry shells and arrange the garnish on top.

Combine the oil and vinegar to make a dressing. Serve salad leaves, tossed in the dressing, on each plate and place a tart beside the leaves, sprinkling a few more drops of dressing around the plate.

Serves 6

An Súgán, well known for its seafood, in Clonakilty, Co. Cork

DEVILED SHRIMP

"Devils," highly spiced morsels of fish or fowl, were hugely popular in Ireland in the past, for supper or after dinner, when they were considered as a stimulant to the punch bowl, or before dinner, as a spur to a jaded appetite. Numerous recipes for the definitive "devil" were exchanged, many of tear-compelling pungency.

12 large raw shrimp
1 teaspoon kosher salt
1 teaspoon cayenne pepper
1 teaspoon paprika
1 teaspoon ground cumin
2 tablespoons butter, melted
2 limes or 1 lemon
mustard powder (optional)

Peel the shells from the shrimps but leave the tails intact.

To make the "devil," mix the salt and spices together and form into a paste with the melted butter, the grated zest of 1 lime or ½ lemon and a little juice. To make it hotter, add more cayenne or a little mustard powder. Marinate the shrimp in this mixture for a couple of hours.

Cook under a medium-high broiler until the shrimp are cooked and the tail shells are pink. Garnish with lime or lemon slices. If using cooked shrimp, broil them just sufficiently to heat thorough.

Serves 4

BLACK "PUDDING" PATTIES

*In Ireland, blood sausages, made with pig's blood, suet, and oatmeal, are
called black puddings.*

12 ounce Clonakilty or other
black pudding
8 ounce freshly cooked
potato
4 scallions, finely chopped
1 egg, beaten
1 large cooking apple, peeled
and grated or chopped
4 tablespoons butter
milk (optional)
2 tablespoons whole-wheat
flour
3 tablespoons oil for frying
2 large eating apples
small glass of white wine,
vermouth, or stock
salt and freshly ground
black pepper
arugula or watercress, to
garnish

Peel the casing from the black
pudding and finely crumble it into a
mixing bowl. Mash in the potato,
scallions, grated apple, half the
butter, and the egg. Mix well
together and form into 12 patties,
adding a tablespoon or so of milk
if the mixture is too dry. Dust with
the flour and fry gently in the oil
until hot and crisp; keep warm.

Wash the eating apples and cut
across into 1/2-inch slices. Stamp
out the cores. In another pan, fry
the apple slices in the remaining
butter until beginning to brown
but not breaking up.
Arrange these on the plates, 2 per
person and place the patties on
top. Pour the wine into the pan
and bubble well to deglaze the
pan. Pour the juices around the
patties. Garnish with the arugula,
watercress, or other leaves.

Serves 6

Conor Pass on the Dingle Peninsula

CHESTNUT AND LENTIL SOUP

This lovely soup is redolent of the season, with its warm color and earthy flavors. A glass of not too dry sherry, an amontillado, perhaps, is excellent with this, a fashion due for revival.

2 bacon slices, finely chopped
2 large onions, finely chopped
2 garlic cloves, finely chopped
4 tablespoons butter
3 celery sticks, with leaves, chopped
1 carrot, grated
8 ounce prepared chestnuts (see page 84)
1¹/₂ cups green or brown lentils
1 teaspoon ground cumin
5 cups chicken or vegetable stock
salt and freshly ground black pepper
²/₃ cup whipping cream, to serve

Put the bacon, onions, and garlic in a large saucepan with the butter and sauté until the bacon is cooked and the onions are soft. Add the celery (reserve the leaves) and carrot and cook 3 to 4 minutes. Purée the cooked chestnuts in a blender with 4 tablespoons of water and stir into the pan.

Add the lentils, cumin, and the stock to the pan and simmer until the lentils are soft. Reserve 1 to 2 cupfuls of the soup, to give a little texture, and purée the remainder. Return to the reserved soup and season well.

Reheat and serve with a spoonful of cream in each bowl, and the chopped celery leaves (or parsley) sprinkled over the tops.

Serves 6

FALL
main courses

BRAISED PHEASANTS WITH IRISH WHISKEY SAUCE

Pheasants are in season from October to January and are usually plentiful during this period.
Braising the birds keeps them moist and tender.

2 pheasants
6 tablespoons butter
6 celery sticks, roughly chopped
4 carrots, roughly chopped
4 onions, roughly chopped
fresh parsley and thyme sprigs
1¼ cups chicken stock
4 tablespoons red-currant jelly
large glass of Irish whiskey
1¼ cups whipping cream
salt and freshly ground black pepper

FOR THE STUFFING
1 cup hazelnuts
1 tablespoon butter
1 tablespoon each finely chopped carrot, celery, and onion
2 bacon slices, chopped
1 orange
6 tablespoons cooked wild and long-grain rice mixture
1 tablespoon Irish whiskey

chestnuts and game chips, to garnish (optional, see below)

To make the stuffing, lightly brown the hazelnuts in a heavy pan. Rub off any loose skins and chop finely. In the same pan, melt 2 tablespoons butter and sauté the chopped vegetables and bacon. Grate the zest of the orange and mix with the other ingredients, rice, and remaining butter. Moisten with 1 tablespoon each whiskey and orange juice. Season well. When the mixture is cold, stuff the birds loosely and secure closed with a wooden toothpick.

In a heavy flameproof casserole that will just fit the 2 birds, melt 4 tablespoons butter and brown the birds all over; remove. Put in the roughly chopped vegetables and a few sprigs of parsley and thyme. Lay the birds on top, on their sides, and pour the stock over.

Season the birds well. Cover the casserole, sealing it well with foil, if necessary. Cook gently 20 minutes, then turn the pheasants and cook 15 to 20 minutes longer. Test by inserting a skewer between the leg and the breast; the liquid should be faintly pink—pheasants do not benefit from overcooking. Remove the birds and keep them warm.

Strain the liquid from the vegetables and remove as much fat as possible. Blend the liquid with the red-currant jelly and pour into a small saucepan. Add the whiskey and heat for a few moments. Ignite to burn off the alcohol and concentrate the flavor. Stir in the cream, taste for seasoning, and boil hard to reduce. Finally, whisk in a little butter.

Arrange the birds on a serving dish, tuck the feathers under the tails (see photograph), if you have them, and glaze with a little sauce.

In Ireland, pheasants are traditionally garnished with chestnuts and game chips, or served on a bed of spinach, finished in butter and garlic.

Game chips are made by slicing peeled potatoes very thinly into cold water. Remove from the water, dry, and fry in hot oil. Drain and sprinkle with salt.

Note: to prepare chestnuts, make a cross in the skins with a sharp knife and boil for 20 minutes; cool and peel. Return to the water and continue cooking until tender.

Serves 4 to 6 (large cock pheasants will serve 3 people generously)

Caherciveen on the Ring of Kerry

LAMB WITH CRABAPPLE JELLY

Crabapples can often be found for the taking, in woodland areas and along roadsides. They are abundant in Killarney, and their wild and winey flavor gives character to this simple sauce. Ordinary apple jelly can be enhanced by the addition of a little red-currant jelly.

1 to 2 racks of lamb (4 to 6 cutlets each; hotel racks)
3 tablespoons olive oil
large glass each of red wine and stock or water
3 large garlic cloves
2 to 3 fresh rosemary sprigs or 1 teaspoon dried rosemary
2 tablespoons dried pink peppercorns
3 tablespoons crabapple jelly
lemon juice, if necessary
2 tablespoons butter, chilled and diced
sea salt and freshly ground black pepper
fresh rosemary sprigs, to garnish

Trim the lamb of any excess fat and neatly pare the bones. Season with black pepper and rub over with some of the olive oil. Place in a deep dish and pour the wine and stock or water over. Crush the garlic cloves and tuck them, with the rosemary, into the meat. Marinate for half an hour or so, or overnight.

To cook, preheat the oven to 425°F. Remove the meat and blot dry with paper towels. In a hot pan, brown the end chops in the remaining oil. Rub a little more oil over the meat and sprinkle the skin with salt. Roast for about 15 minutes for pink lamb; 5 minutes or so longer if you prefer it nearing well done. Transfer the lamb to a dish, cover with foil and a towel and leave to rest.

Strain the marinade into a saucepan. Add a sprig of rosemary and the pink peppercorns (if you can only find the brined sort, rise off the brine and use only 1 tablespoon). Boil rapidly to reduce; then add the crabapple jelly, whisking well to dissolve. Taste, adding a little lemon juice if it's too sweet. Pour any juices from the roasting pan into the sauce, remove the rosemary, and whisk in the butter, a piece at a time.

Slice the lamb into chops, 2 or 3 per person, depending on size. Pour a small pool of sauce on each plate and arrange the chops on top. Garnish with the rosemary sprigs.

Serves 4 to 6

A disused shed in Co. Wexford

PORK AND APPLE PIE

This pie is based on one given by Hannah Glasse in her famous 1758 cookbook,
The Art of Cookery made Plain and Easy. *This book circulated so widely
in Ireland it was said to be the only book in some houses of the day.*

2 large onions, finely chopped

2 tablespoons butter

2 pounds good sausage meat
   or equal quantities of pork
   pieces and belly of pork,
   finely ground

1 cup finely chopped bacon

1¹/₂ pounds apples, peeled,
   cored, and chopped

2 tablespoons brown sugar

2 to 3 fresh sage leaves,
   chopped, or a little dried sage

5 to 6 juniper berries

glass of white wine or hard
   cider

salt, freshly ground black
   pepper, and grated nutmeg

1 egg, beaten, to glaze

FOR THE PASTRY

3 cups all-purpose flour

1 cup (2 sticks) butter

1 egg

1 to 2 tablespoons very cold
   water

salt, pinch

Make the pastry dough in the
usual way (see page 80) adding an
egg as well as water, and roll out
two-thirds to line a greased 9-inch
square cake pan. Roll out the
remainder to make the lid. Chill
for at least 30 minutes.

Preheat the oven to 350°F. Sauté
the onions in half the butter until
soft. Cool and add to the sausage
meat, bacon, apples, and sugar.
Season well with pepper, salt, and

a good grating of nutmeg. Add the
sage (be sparing if it is dried).
Spread the meat in the dough
case, pushing the juniper berries
down into the mixture. Pour the
wine or cider over and dot with
the remaining butter. If pork is
used, add a little more butter
(about 4 tablespoons). Cover with
the dough lid, dampening and
pressing the edges well together.
Brush the top with the beaten egg.

Bake for about 1 hour, covering
the top with foil if it's getting too
brown. Cool on a wire rack.

When cold, cut into squares and
serve with a green salad, fruity
chutney, and good bread.

Serves 4

ROAST MICHAELMAS GOOSE WITH PRUNE, APPLE, AND POTATO STUFFING

The tradition of a goose for dinner on the feast of St. Michael (29th September) is as old as that of the Christmas goose, and made good sense: the spring geese were turned out to fatten among the stubble after the grain was harvested, making them comfortably plump for Michaelmas.

**10 to 12 pound goose (reserve
  the giblets for stock)**
1 onion, sliced
1 tablespoon butter
**12 ounce prunes, soaked
  and chopped**
2³/₄ cups chopped apples
1³/₄ cups mashed potatoes
1 teaspoon caraway seeds
1 tablespoon Dijon mustard
1 tablespoon orange zest
**1 tablespoon chopped fresh
  sage or ¹/₂ teaspoon dried**
1 tablespoon kosher salt
freshly ground black pepper

To drain some of the fat and dry the skin in readiness for its roasting crisply, prick the goose thoroughly all over with a fork. Pour boiling water over the skin and leave to dry in an airy place while you make the stuffing.

Cook the onion in the butter until soft. Mix with the chopped prunes, apples, and mashed potato. Add the caraway seeds, mustard, orange zest, and herbs; season well.

When ready to cook, dry the goose skin with paper towels and rub well with salt. Pack the stuffing loosely into the cavity and put any surplus into a foil-covered dish to cook separately.

Preheat the oven to 425°F. Secure the legs in place by passing a skewer through the first joint of one leg through to the other leg, or tie securely in place.

Sit the goose, breast down, on a rack in a deep roasting pan. Roast for 40 minutes, then lower the heat to 300°F, turning the goose breast side up at the half way point. Allow about 20 minutes to the pound. Test by inserting a skewer between the leg and the breast; clear liquid indicates the bird is done. There will be a great deal of fat, so pour it off once or twice during cooking. Treasure the fat for roasting potatoes.

When the goose is ready, cover it with foil and a towel to rest for at least 30 minutes.

To make the gravy, add a little stock (made with the giblets) and a glass of wine or 2 tablespoons orange juice to the de-fatted sediment in the roasting pan, scraping it up well. Boil to reduce, then whisk in a little butter.

Serve with Sautéed Cabbage (page 90).

Serves 6

A lane in Lauragh, Co. Kerry

SAUTÉED CABBAGE WITH BACON

8 ounce slab bacon, cubed

2 tablespoons oil

2 tablespoons wine vinegar

6 tablespoons water

1 teaspoon sugar

1 teaspoon caraway seeds

2^1/$_2$ cups finely sliced or
   shredded cabbage, hard
   stalks removed

1 large cooking apple, peeled
   and chopped

salt and freshly ground
   black pepper

Cook the bacon cubes in the oil in
a large pan until crisp; remove and
keep warm. Add the vinegar, water,
sugar, and caraway seeds to the
pan, scraping up the sediment, and
boil for a few moments.

Add the cabbage and apple to
the pan and cook, stirring
frequently, until the cabbage is just
tender and the apple soft and
melting, 7 to 8 minutes. Taste for
seasoning. Sprinkle the bacon on
top and serve.

This dish is excellent with fowl
and game.

Serves 6 as a side dish

CHICKEN HOT POT WITH CASHEW NUTS

This chicken pie is ideal comfort food for cold evenings. The cashews can be replaced by the more traditional toasted whole almonds.

1 onion, chopped

3 carrots

1 bay leaf

3 cups water

2 celery sticks

4 large skinned chicken
  breasts

2 chicken legs

1 tablespoon oil

³/₄ cup cashew nuts

8 shallots, peeled

chopped fresh or dried
  tarragon

2 tablespoons all-purpose
  flour

2 tablespoons butter

salt, freshly ground black
  pepper, and grated nutmeg

FOR THE TOPPING

1¹/₂ pounds potatoes

2 tablespoons butter

hot milk

Put the onion, 1 carrot, and the bay leaf in the water and cook for 40 minutes to make a stock. Strain. Cut the remaining carrots and the celery into thick slices and add with the chicken to the stock. Simmer until the vegetables are cooked but still crisp; remove with a slotted spoon. Remove the breasts as soon as they are just cooked, after 12 to 15 minutes, and continue cooking until the legs are tender. Skin and bone the chicken legs and put the meat with the breasts. Return the trimmings to the stock and boil hard to reduce to about 2¹/₂ cups.

In a small pan, heat the oil. Add the nuts and toast for a few moments. Remove the nuts and cook the shallots in the same pan, until they are nicely browned. Add a ladleful of stock and cook until they are tender. Arrange the nuts,

vegetables, and chicken, which has been cut into nice pieces, in a deep baking dish suitable for serving from. Season well. Add a little chopped fresh tarragon, less if using dried.

Cook the flour in the melted butter in a large saucepan. Gradually stir in the strained hot stock, stirring until the sauce thickens. Season well with salt, pepper, and nutmeg and pour over the chicken and vegetables in the pie dish; set aside. Preheat the oven to 400°F.

Boil the potatoes in their skins until tender. Mash thoroughly, adding the butter and enough hot milk to make them creamy. Spread, or pipe over the dish. Bake in the top of the oven until the sauce is bubbling and the potatoes are golden brown. Follow with a salad.

Serves 4 to 6

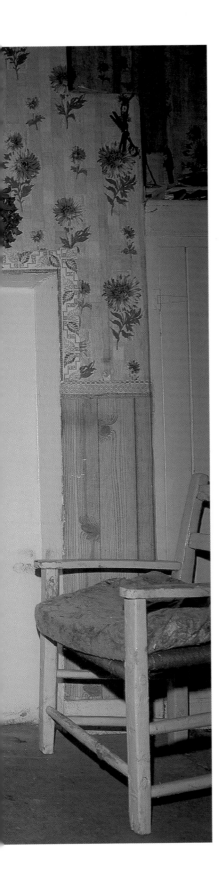

Open fire in a Lixnaw cottage, north Kerry

COLCANNON

Although variations of colcannon are eaten all year round,
it always forms part of the Hallowe'en table.
Originally the centerpiece of a meatless, fast-day supper,
nowadays, it more often accompanies roasts.

1 pound kale or green
cabbage
1¹/₂ pounds potatoes,
unpeeled
1 bunch scallions, finely
chopped
³/₄ cup whipping cream, hot
or milk
¹/₂ cup (1 stick) butter
salt and white pepper

Remove the hard stems from the kale or cabbage, and cook in salted, boiling water until tender—kale takes a surprisingly long time, about 25 minutes; cabbage will take less. Drain, press out any remaining water and chop finely.

Boil the potatoes in another pan of salted, boiling water until soft; drain and dry over the heat for a few minutes, covered with a dish towel. Peel and mash carefully by hand, removing any lumps; do not use a food processor. The scallions can be cooked in the cream or milk for a few minutes, but I prefer them raw. Add them to the potatoes, with the hot cream or milk, half the butter, and the kale. Mix thoroughly together. Check and adjust the seasoning. Put into a large serving bowl and make a well in the middle to hold the remaining butter. Serve very hot.

Rings, well wrapped, can be inserted for Hallowe'en (see Fall introduction).

Serves 4

Bunratty Folk Park, Co. Clare

COLCANNON—
A WEXFORD
VERSION

*Almost every region of Ireland
has its version of colcannon and
each claims theirs as the "true"
recipe. Like traditional dishes
worldwide, the local version
contains whatever is readily
available. Wexford's comfortable
farms were known for their
vegetable gardens and orchards.*

8 large potatoes, peeled
1 large parsnip, peeled
1 large onion
1 cabbage or kale
$^1/_2$ cup (1 stick) butter
hot milk
bunch fresh parsley, chopped
salt and freshly ground
 black pepper
chopped fresh parsley or
 chopped scallions, to garnish

 Rinse, dry, and chop all the
vegetables into small pieces,
keeping one large cabbage or kale
leaf aside. Place them in a steamer
or colander over boiling water.
Cover with the cabbage leaf and
the lid and steam for 45 minutes
to 1 hour until all the vegetables
are tender. Mash the potatoes and
vegetables together, with the
parsley. Season with pepper and
salt and add 6 tablespoons butter
and sufficient hot milk to make a
creamy texture.
 Serve in a mound on a deep
dish with the remaining butter
pressed into the middle and
chopped parsley or scallions
scattered over the top.
 Serves 4

RABBIT WITH ALMONDS

*Rabbit, like chicken today, was immensely popular in the past.
Dozens of recipes survive from Irish household recipe books. Almonds,
too, were widely used for flavor and texture in a variety of dishes.
Rabbit meat is extremely lean, which makes it ideal for contemporary
tastes, and today's tender rabbits are specially bred for the table. Wild
rabbits take longer to cook and have a gamier flavor.*

2½ to 3 pounds rabbit,
  cut into 8 to 10 pieces
1½ cups blanched whole
  almonds
1 tablespoon vinegar
1 tablespoon salt
2 tablespoons all-purpose
  flour
2 tablespoons butter
1 tablespoon oil
2 onions, sliced
1 cup chopped bacon
2 tablespoons Irish whiskey
sprig fresh thyme
1 bay leaf
glass of white wine
glass of stock or water
grated zest and juice of
  1 lemon
salt and freshly ground
  black pepper

Soak the rabbit for several hours in water, with the vinegar and salt. If the rabbit is wild, soak overnight.

Preheat the oven to 350°F. Remove the rabbit from the water, rinse well, and pat dry. Season the pieces and flour well. Brown the rabbit in the butter and oil in a flameproof casserole. Add the onions and bacon and continue cooking until they soften slightly. Add the whiskey and when it has just warmed, ignite it. When the flames die down add the lemon juice and zest, almonds, wine, and stock or water. Check the seasoning.

Cover tightly and transfer to the oven (it can also remain on top of the stove, if more convenient). Cook for about 1 hour. Test with a skewer for tenderness and add a little more wine or stock if the rabbit needs more cooking or the sauce seems to be dry.

Serve the rabbit arranged on a dish of plain boiled rice. Pour the pan juices over.

Serves 4

Roundstone Harbor, Co. Galway

BAKED COD
WITH
MUSHROOMS

1 medium onion
1 leek, cleaned
4 tablespoons butter
4 to 6 cod steaks or fillets
3^1/$_2$ cups diced mushrooms
grated zest of ^{1}/$_2$ lemon
1^1/$_3$ tablespoons all-purpose
  flour
1^1/$_4$ cups fish stock or milk, hot
6 canned anchovy fillets, split
  in half (optional)
^{1}/$_2$ cup fresh bread crumbs
salt and freshly ground
  black pepper
chopped fresh parsley, to
  garnish

Preheat the oven to 325°F. Chop
the onion finely and slice the leek.
Cook them slowly in half the
butter until soft. Spread in a
buttered baking dish suitable for
serving from. Place the seasoned
fish on top.

  Melt the remaining butter and
cook the mushrooms and lemon
zest for several minutes until the
juices run and the mushrooms are
beginning to brown. Add the flour
and stir well until the flour is
cooked, 2 to 3 minutes. Gradually
stir in the stock or milk, stirring well
to prevent lumps from forming.

  Pour the sauce over the fish and
leek mixture. If you are using
anchovies, arrange them on top of
the sauce. Sprinkle the bread
crumbs over the top. Bake 25
minutes. Serve hot, straight from
the dish.

  Serves 4 to 6

FALL
desserts

FALL APPLE TART

Armagh has been renowned for more than 200 years for the quality of her apples. This tart combines two types of apple, cooking apples for the purée, and eating apples, which hold their shape when cooked, for the apple slices. The tart can be garnished with whatever fresh fruit is in season.

FOR THE PASTRY
1 cup plus 2 tablespoons flour
2 tablespoons superfine sugar
¹/₂ cup (1 stick) butter, chilled and diced
1 egg yolk
1 tablespoon lemon juice
salt

FOR THE FILLING
3 large cooking apples, such as Bramley or Courtlands
3 large red eating apples, such as Fuji or McIntosh
1 tablespoon grated lemon zest
superfine sugar, to taste
1 tablespoon lemon juice
1 tablespoon butter, melted
2 tablespoons confectioners' sugar

To make the pastry, sift the flour with a pinch of salt. Stir in the sugar. Rub the butter into the flour and salt with your fingertips, or pulse in the food processor. Beat the egg yolk with the lemon juice and mix into the dough. Add a few drops more cold water if required. Roll out or pat into a greased 9-inch tart pan with a removable bottom. Chill for an hour.

Preheat the oven to 375°F. Peel and core the cooking apples. Cook slowly until soft, adding a spoonful of water if necessary. Press through a strainer or purée. Add the lemon zest and sweeten to taste with superfine sugar. When cold, spread over the dough in the pan.

Quarter and core the unpeeled red apples, cut into neat slices, and brush with lemon juice. Arrange the slices in a circle around the pan, on top of the purée, covering it completely. Brush the slices with melted butter and sprinkle a little confectioners' sugar over the top, using a fine sifter.

Cover the apple slices with a circle of foil for the first 15 minutes of baking. Bake about 35 minutes until the pastry has shrunk a little from the sides of the pan and the apples are slightly tinged with color. Serve warm or cold.

Serves 6

Near Glencar, Co. Kerry

GREEN FOOL

The creamy unctuous qualities of the avocado are not utilized sufficiently in sweet dishes. Combined here with the last of the summer gooseberries it brings new life to a classic gooseberry fool.

1¹/₂ pounds gooseberries
1 large, ripe avocado, peeled,
** pitted, and chopped**
sugar
grated zest and juice of 1 lime

Wash and top and tail the gooseberries. Cook until soft; this can be done in the oven or gently on the stove, but the microwave is ideal because the berries keep their color.

Purée the gooseberries in a food processor and strain to remove the seeds. Return the purée to the processor with the avocado and blend until creamy; the avocado will discolor quickly, so sprinkle a little of the lime juice over it first.

Sweeten the purée to your taste with the sugar. Add the lime zest and the juice of half the lime. Chill for at least an hour. Serve in glasses, with pretty cookies.
Serves 4

FALL PUDDING

This is a fall version of summer pudding, a sort of consolation for the passing of the brilliant summer raspberries and red currants. In its own way, it's just as nice. The traditional combination is apples, plums (peeled, pitted, and cut into small cubes), and blackberries. The bread should be stale, at least two days old and anything from sliced pan to brioche is suitable, if it can be cut to shape. The loaf-style Barm Brack (see page 105) is excellent. Homemade custard sauce, hot or cold, or whipped cream mixed with crème fraîche or sour cream, are equally good with this.

2 pounds mixed fruit, such as apples, plums, blackberries, and fall rhubarb, prepared as necessary
sugar, to taste
8 to 10 stale bread slices

Cook the fruit gently in a pan, using as little water as possible to moisten it (1 to 2 tablespoons at most) or, better still, cook it in the microwave, until just soft and the juices are just beginning to run. Sweeten to taste.

Butter a deep 5-cup bowl or Irish pudding basin. Cut a circle from one slice of bread to fit the bottom of the bowl, then cut the rest into sections to fit the sides, reserving some for the top. Gently spoon in the hot fruit, arrange the lid pieces to fit tightly, then cover with baking parchment or foil. Put a small plate or saucer on top and weigh it down with a can so that the juices seep into the bread; keep any juice which spills over. Leave the pudding to cool, then refrigerate overnight.

To serve, run a round-bladed knife around the edge between the bread and the bowl and turn out on to a deep plate. Pour any remaining juices over the top.

Serves 4 to 5

APPLE DUMPLINGS

"C— holds that a man cannot have a pure mind who refuses apple dumplings. I am not certain but he is right."
Charles Lamb, The Essays of Elia

6 large eating apples, such as Fuji or McIntosh
1¹/₂ pounds piecrust dough or puff pastry dough, home-made or commercial
2 tablespoons lemon juice
5 sticks rhubarb or 1 pound plums, pitted, or a mixture of both
2 tablespoons golden raisins
³/₄ cup light brown sugar
6 cloves
5 tablespoons butter
1 egg, beaten

Preheat the oven to 350°F. Peel the apples and brush with lemon juice. Remove the cores and a little of the apple to enlarge the cavities. Rinse and chop the rhubarb or plums. Combine with the removed apple and golden raisins and heat slowly in 2 tablespoons butter until soft but not mushy. Fill the apples with the fruit mixture, sweeten to taste, and add a clove to each. Top with ¹/₂ tablespoon butter.

Cut the dough into 6 pieces and roll them out until they are large enough to enclose the apples. Set each apple on a square of dough and damp the edges. Draw up the corners, cut away the surplus dough, and press the edges well together, molding to fit the apples. Roll out the dough trimmings to make leaves and use these to cover any imperfections. Make a steam hole in the top of each, brush with the beaten egg and then sprinkle with sugar.

Bake about 45 minutes until the pastry is golden brown; very large apples may take a little longer. A skewer pressed into the side will tell if it is tender.

Cooking apples can be used for apple dumplings if you like tart flavors, but add extra sugar. Vanilla ice cream is very good with apple dumplings.

Serves 6

A house with a view near Kenmare on the Ring of Kerry

ORANGE–CARAWAY CAKE

Caraway seeds, and ginger, have been intensively used in Irish cooking since at least the seventeenth century and are just as popular today. This variation on the seed, or Madeira, cake is very good. Without the orange and marmalade, this recipe makes an excellent plain seed cake, which was always on hand to offer with a glass of sherry or Madeira when friends called.

$^1/_2$ **cup (1 stick) butter, softened**
$^1/_2$ **cup light brown sugar**
2 extra-large eggs
2 tablespoons orange marmalade
1 tablespoon caraway seeds
grated zest and juice of 1 orange
1$^1/_2$ cups all-purpose flour
1$^1/_4$ teaspoons baking powder
2 tablespoons confectioners' sugar, sifted
salt, pinch

Preheat the oven to 325°F. Sift the flour with the baking powder and salt. Cream the butter and the sugar until light and fluffy and pale in color. Add the eggs, beating them in one at a time, adding 1 tablespoon of flour with each. Add the marmalade, caraway seeds, and orange zest and juice.

Fold the remaining flour into the batter. Pour into a well-greased 9-inch mold. Bake for about 45 minutes until it has shrunk slightly from the sides of the tin. Cool slightly before turning out. When cool, dredge the cake with confectioners' sugar.

CINNAMON TOAST

A teatime treat from times past when toast was made in front of the fire. It tastes just as good today.

thick slices of white bread
butter
ground cinnamon
light brown sugar

Toast one side of the bread. Butter the untoasted side generously, sprinkle liberally with the cinnamon and then the sugar. Brown under the broiler and eat immediately, while the buttery cinnamon runs down your chin.

Araglin Forest Park on the Dingle Peninsula

F A L L
baking

MARBLE CAKE

Marble cake has fascinated children for generations and it is
always a popular feature of the Irish tea table.

**1 cup plus 2 tablespoons all-
purpose flour**
1 teaspoon baking powder
salt
**3 ounce bittersweet chocolate
or 1 tablespoon unsweetened
cocoa powder mixed with
2 tablespoons milk**
**³/₄ cup (1¹/₂ sticks) butter,
softened**
**³/₄ cup plus 2 tablespoons
superfine sugar**
3 extra-large eggs
**grated zest and juice of
1 lemon**

Preheat the oven to 325°F. Sift the
flour with the baking powder and a
pinch of salt. Melt the chocolate, if
using, over hot water.

Beat the butter in a large bowl
until soft. Add the sugar and
continue beating until the mixture
is pale and creamy. Add the eggs,
one by one, adding a spoonful of

flour with each and beating well
after each egg. Fold and cut in the
remaining flour carefully in a couple
of batches, making sure no pockets
of flour remain. Divide the mixture,
putting half into another bowl. To
this add the lemon zest and 1 to 2
tablespoons juice, to your taste. To
the other bowl add the chocolate
or cocoa mixture, mixing it in
gently but thoroughly.

Drop the batters into a buttered
and lined 9-x 5-inch bread pan, 3
spoonfuls of one and then the
other until you have used all of
both batters. Draw a knife through
the mixture diagonally from each
end of the pan to create an
attractive marbled effect.

Bake for 45 minutes, or until the
cake has shrunk slightly from the
sides of the pan. Cover with foil if
the top is browning too quickly.
Leave to cool briefly in the pan,
then transfer to a wire rack.

MACAROONS

*These classic macaroons were an
important component of the
"biscuit tin," to be offered with
a glass of sherry or a cup of tea.*

2 extra-large egg whites
1 cup blanched almonds, very
  finely ground
almond or ratafia extract
1 cup plus 2 tablespoons
  superfine sugar
$1/4$ cup rice flour
rice paper
slivered almonds

Preheat the oven to 350°F.
Line a buttered baking tray with
rice paper. Lightly whisk the egg
whites with a fork.

Mix the ground almonds, extract,
sugar, and rice flour together. Stir in
the whites thoroughly. Using a
teaspoon, drop spoonfuls of the
mixture onto the rice paper, well
apart. Top each with an almond
sliver and bake until golden brown,
8 to 10 minutes. Transfer, still on the
rice paper, to a rack to cool. Tear or
cut away the excess paper from
the edges of the cookies. The rice
paper is, of course, edible. If you
use non-edible parchment paper,
however, remember to remove it.
Makes about 20

Caherconree, Iveragh Peninsula

WALNUT CAKE

1³/₄ cups all-purpose flour
scant ¹/₂ cup walnuts
scant 1 cup butter, softened
³/₄ cup plus 2 tablespoons
  superfine sugar
4 extra-large eggs, at room
  temperature
1 teaspoon vanilla extract
grated zest and juice of a
  lemon
confectioners' sugar and extra
  lemon juice for frosting
  (optional)

Preheat the oven to 350°F. Butter
and line a 9- × 5-inch bread pan.
Sift the flour; set aside. Crumble
the walnuts with your fingers.

In a large bowl, cream the butter.
Add the sugar, beating until pale
and creamy. Add the eggs, one by
one, adding 1 tablespoon flour and
beating between each.

Stir in the walnuts, vanilla, and 1
tablespoon lemon juice. Beat them
in well and then fold in the
remaining flour, in 3 parts, cutting it
in rather than beating it, but making
sure no flour pockets remain.

Transfer the batter to the
prepared pan and sprinkle the top
with lemon zest. Place a piece of
foil loosely over the top and bake
for about an hour, lowering the
heat to 325°F and removing the
foil after half an hour. Bake until the
cake shrinks slightly from the sides
of the pan. When baked, cool
slightly in the pan before transfering
to a wire rack to cool completely.

The cake can be frosted with a
little confectioners' sugar, mixed
with 1 tablespoon of lemon juice
and spread over the top. The cake
will keep for a few days in an
airtight container.

BARM BRACK

The barm brack (barm is the yeasty ferment produced when brewing ale or beer; brack, or breac, refers to its speckled nature) is one of the few Irish traditional breads or cakes raised with yeast, and, like hot-cross buns, the origins are lost in antiquity. It is an essential part of the Hallowe'en festivities and usually contains a ring—whoever gets the ring will be married within the year.

3³/₄ cups all-purpose flour

4 to 5 saffron strands

2 tablespoons water

1 teaspoon salt

4 tablespoons brown sugar

2 teaspoons apple-pie
  spice, or to taste

1 envelope quick-rising active
  dry yeast

6 tablespoons butter, diced

2 cups mixed dried fruit
  and chopped candied peel

2 eggs, beaten

1¹/₄ cups milk, warm

TO GLAZE

1 tablespoon sugar

4 tablespoons water

Put the saffron to soak in the water for 15 minutes. In a large bowl, mix the flour, salt, sugar, spice, and dry yeast together. Rub in the butter and then add the fruit and peel. Add the beaten eggs and the saffron mixture to the warm milk. Make a well in the flour mixture and pour in the liquid, reserving 1 tablespoon. Mix well together, drawing in the flour from the sides. When the mixture will hold

together, turn out and knead 5 to 6 minutes. Return to the bowl and cover with plastic wrap. Leave to rise in a warm place until doubled in bulk.

Grease two 8-inch cake pans 3 inch deep and, if you like, wrap 2 inexpensive rings in greaseproof paper. Turn out the dough and knead again briefly; then divide between the cake pans. Press the rings into the middle. Leave to rise for 30 minutes longer.

Preheat the oven to 425°F. Brush the cakes with the reserved liquid and bake for 10 minutes; then reduce the heat to 375°F and bake until the bottom sounds hollow when tapped, 40 to 50 minutes.

Make a glaze with the sugar and water by dissolving the sugar in the water, and boiling until reduced. Brush over the bracks and return to the oven to set for 5 minutes.

Lough Delphi, Co. Mayo. Overleaf: Brandon Mountain, Co. Kerry

WINTER

WITH Hallowe'en past and the gardens tidied up and put to bed, the focus turns to Christmas. The preparation of cakes and puddings usually began in November and it was the custom for everyone living in the house to stir the plum pudding for luck.

This was an invariable rule in my own home and there was a vague dread in our minds, as children, that if everyone didn't stir it something might happen to the pudding: a disaster, since it was the thing we liked best for the Christmas feast.

Christmas is still an intensely family affair in Ireland and the prospect of children home from school and perhaps friends or family home from abroad brings an air of excitement to the preparations. Turkey is the most popular centerpiece of the Christmas dinner, although many people still prefer goose, and there is always a splendid ham to partner the turkey, and spiced beef to hand around with drinks. On Christmas Eve, candles are still lit in the windows to welcome the Holy Family and guide them to rest. The Feast of the Epiphany, January 6, is known in Ireland as Little Christmas or *Nollaig na mBan*, Women's Christmas, when women had their own feast with all the dishes dear to their hearts. This excellent custom, although rather in abeyance for some years, is now happily enjoying a revival.

OYSTERS IN CHAMPAGNE SAUCE

The charm of this dish lies in the combination of the hot sauce with the cold oysters, the perfect introduction to the Christmas dinner. The sauce can be made in advance and reheated.

24 oysters

3 shallots, very finely
  chopped

2 tablespoons butter

1½ tablespoons all-purpose
  flour

glass of champagne or
  white wine

1¼ cups whipping cream

cayenne pepper or Tabasco
  sauce

chopped fresh parsley, to
  garnish

Scrub the oysters thoroughly and soak them in cold water for an hour or so; drain.

Open the oysters carefully (see below), saving as much of their liquid as possible. Put the oysters in the refrigerator while you make the sauce.

Cook the shallots in a pan with the butter until transparent but not brown.

Add the flour and stir well until it is cooked. Add the champagne or wine and the strained oyster liquid to the roux, whisking well to prevent lumps and cooking until reduced somewhat, 5 or 6 minutes. Gradually stir in the cream and simmer for a few moments. Simmer gently until the sauce reduces and thickens sufficiently. Season to your taste with the cayenne or Tabasco—it probably won't need salt.(Use paprika if cayenne is too hot.)

When you are ready to serve, arrange the oysters on plates and put a spoonful of the hot sauce over each cold oyster. Garnish with parsley.

Note: to open an oyster, hold it firmly in your left hand and insert a short sharp knife near the hinge, working it from right to left until the muscle is severed. Prise the oyster open.

Serves 4

Gathering seaweed, Brandon Bay, Co. Kerry. Previous pages: Conor Pass, Co. Kerry.

SMOKED FISH TART WITH ARDRAHAN CHEESE

Combining Ardrahan cheese, from Kanturk, Co. Cork, with smoked fish, is the inspirational idea of Geert Maes, chef patron of Gaby's Restaurant in Killarney, one of Ireland's most respected restaurants. If Ardrahan cheese is unavailable, use Gruyere or an aged Gouda.

FOR THE PASTRY

$^1/_2$ **cup (1 stick) butter**

$1^1/_3$ **cups all-purpose flour**

$^1/_4$ **teaspoon salt**

1 egg yolk

1 to 2 tablespoons very cold water, if necessary

FOR THE FILLING

1 onion, chopped

1 carrot, chopped

$^1/_2$ **tablespoon oil**

1 bay leaf

black peppercorns

8 ounce smoked haddock or cod

4 ounce Ardrahan cheese

4 extra-large eggs

$1^1/_4$ **cups whipping cream**

freshly ground black pepper and grated nutmeg

Preheat the oven to 400°F. To make the dough, rub the butter into the sifted flour and salt. Moisten with the egg yolk, adding 1 tablespoon or so of cold water if required. Roll out, or press into a 9-inch round quiche pan, 2-inch deep, with a removable bottom.

Chill until required.

Soften the onion and carrot in the oil. Add the bay leaf, peppercorns, and enough water just to cover. Boil about 10 minutes. Gently poach the fish in this stock until tender and the flesh flakes, 5 to 6 minutes. Take out the fish, flake and remove any bones or hard pieces; keep the stock for soups.

Using a potato peeler, remove the thin outer rind from the Ardrahan cheese and then cut the cheese into thin slices. Arrange these on the bottom of the dough and put the flaked fish on top.

Beat the eggs and cream together and season well with black pepper and a pinch of nutmeg; it probably won't need salt. Pour into the dough. Bake for about 40 minutes until golden on top and the pastry has shrunk slightly away from the sides of the tin. Reduce the oven to 300°F after 5 minutes.

Serves 6 as an appetizer, 4 as a main course

Kinvara village, Co. Galway

WALNUT SOUP WITH WALNUT AND WATERCRESS SANDWICHES

This simple soup is best made in the winter, when the new season's nuts are fresh. Good homemade stock will also greatly add to the flavor. This soup is particularly popular with men—perhaps because it was frequently served in conjunction with game.

1 cup shelled walnuts
1 large garlic clove
3 cups chicken stock
1¼ cups whipping cream
grated nutmeg
salt and freshly ground
   black pepper
1 tablespoon finely chopped
   fresh chives or parsley, to
   garnish

FOR THE SANDWICH FILLING
½ cup cream cheese
2 tablespoons of finely
   chopped walnuts
2 to 3 tablespoons of chopped
   mustard greens and
   watercress or alfalfa sprouts

To make the soup, crush or blend the walnuts and garlic to a smooth paste, adding a little stock to help it along. Blend in the rest of the stock and cream and season well, grating a very little nutmeg over. Bring to a boil and simmer 4 to 6 minutes before serving. Garnish with the herbs.

To make the sandwich filling, beat together the cream cheese, walnuts, and watercress or sprouts. Spread on thinly-sliced whole-wheat bread.

Serves 4

BAKED EGGS WITH SPINACH

8 ounce spinach
1 tablespoon butter
2 bacon slices
salt and freshly ground black
  pepper
soy sauce
4 extra-large eggs, at room
  temperature
$^{2}/_{3}$ cup whipping cream
chopped fresh chervil

Preheat the oven to 350°F. Wash
the spinach and remove the stems.
Chop coarsely, place in a pan with
the butter, and stew until just
tender. Squeeze out the moisture.

  Cook the bacon until crisp.
Drain and chop finely.

  Butter 4 ramekins. Put 1
tablespoon spinach in each.
Sprinkle the bacon over and
season well, adding a drop or two
of soy sauce. Crack the eggs into
the dishes and cover with the
cream. Sprinkle the chervil over
the tops. Bake 12 to 15 minutes
until the egg whites are set and
the yolks still soft.

  Serves 4

CELERY SOUP WITH BLUE CHEESE

1 large head celery
2 garlic cloves
1 onion
2 tablespoons butter
2 tablespoons all-purpose flour
5 cups vegetable or light chicken stock
²/₃ cups whipping cream
2 to 3 ounce Chetwynde or other good-quality blue cheese, crumbled
2 to 3 scallions, finely chopped, to garnish

Prepare and finely chop the celery, garlic, and onion. Melt the butter in a large saucepan, add the vegetables, and cook stirring frequently, until they begin to soften. Sift in the flour and stir well until it cooks. Gradually add the hot stock, stirring to avoid lumps. Cook 10 minutes or so until the vegetables are very tender. Purée in a blender or food processor.

Return the soup to the saucepan, season well, and stir in the cream. (If it seems too thick, add a little milk also.) Cook a few moments to thicken the cream.

Just before serving, bring back to a boil and stir in the crumbled cheese, but don't continue to boil once the cheese has been added.

Garnish with the scallions. Serve with crusty bread.

Serves 6

Gleann na Gealt (Valley of the Mad Men), Co. Kerry

WINTER
main courses

RAGOUT OF COD AND CLAMS

In the past, clams made only very occasional appearances on our western shores, but in recent years they have been cultivated successfully and have found a natural place in Irish cooking. Basmati rice or new potatoes, buttered and sprinkled with herbs, are good served with this.

2 large onions
1 tablespoon olive oil
2 garlic cloves
3 tablespoons balsamic
  vinegar
1¼ cups fish or chicken
  stock
2 cans crushed Italian
  tomatoes
1 tablespoon chopped fresh
  cilantro
1½ pounds cod
1½ pounds clams
salt and freshly ground
  black pepper

Slice the onions into fine rings. Put them in a heavy, flameproof casserole or saucepan, with the oil and garlic. Sauté gently until they are soft but not brown, then add the balsamic vinegar and the stock. Cover and cook over medium heat until the stock almost evaporates and becomes slightly syrupy; watch it so it doesn't burn. This takes 10 to 15 minutes.

Add the tomatoes and cilantro and cook for 10 minutes more to reduce slightly. Taste for seasoning;

it may not need salt.

Cut the cod into large cubes. Add the cod and clams, still in their shells, to the sauce. Cover and simmer 6 to 7 minutes until the cod is cooked and the clams open; discard any clams that remain closed. Add a few grinds of black pepper and serve.

Serves 6

Roundstone Harbor and the Twelve Pins, Co. Galway

SPICED BEEF

Spiced beef is one of the seasonal pleasures of Christmas. Decorated with holly and embalmed in spice, it can be seen in every butcher's shop during the Christmas season. To make at home, you must start a week or ten days before it is required.

TO PREPARE
4 to 5 pounds beef round, bone removed
1 cup salt
³/₄ cup brown sugar
1 cup apple-pie spice, including mace and nutmeg
2 tablespoons juniper berries, slightly crushed

TO COOK
2 onions, roughly chopped
2 carrots, roughly chopped
2 celery sticks, roughly chopped
2 bay leaves

Mix the dry ingredients together and rub thoroughly into the meat, making sure the bone cavity is well treated. Put the meat in a deep bowl in the refrigerator, and turn it each day, basting well with the liquid which seeps out. After 10 days, it is ready for cooking.

Place the vegetables and bay leaves in a large saucepan and lay the meat on top. Just cover with cold water, bring slowly to a boil, and simmer gently, allowing about 25 minutes per pound.

When cooked, allow the meat to rest in the water for 30 minutes. Transfer to a board. If it is to be eaten cold, usually the case at Christmas, lay another board on top and press overnight with a weight.

Serve cut in very thin slices, with mustard, creamed horseradish, and chutney.

Serves 8 as a main course, 10 to 12 as part of a buffet

VENISON PASTIES

These small pasties are a manageable version of the great decorated venison pies of the past.
These were "sideboard" dishes which allowed the pastry cooks to show off their art.
Widely available, during the winter, both farmed and wild, venison is a lean meat and benefits
from being marinated, which should be as long as time allows.

2 pound breast venison,
  or pieces
2 tablespoons olive oil
2 tablespoons red-wine
  vinegar
2 cloves garlic, crushed
1 glass red wine
ground mace
6 to 7 juniper berries, slightly
  crushed
2 large onions
1 carrot
1 celery stick
4 ounce fatback bacon
2 pounds puff pastry dough,
  thawed if frozen
1 egg, beaten
salt and freshly ground black
  pepper

Cut the venison into cubes and put them in a baking dish, with the oil, vinegar, garlic, wine, and spices to taste. Leave overnight, if possible.

Preheat the oven to 325°F. Chop the vegetables finely. Cut the bacon fat into small cubes and fry until crisp. Add the bacon and vegetables to the meat and marinade, cover and bake 45 minutes to 1 hour, or until the meat is just tender; venison does not benefit from overcooking. Remove and cool.

Turn the oven up to 350°F. Roll out the dough to make 6 pieces, each 6 x 8 inch, patching together if necessary. Pour off and keep any excess juices from the meat filling. Divide the filling between the dough pieces, putting it in the middle and leaving a gap of 2 inches on each side and 1 inch at the top and bottom. Damp the edges with beaten egg and draw the sides together, pinching well. Pinch together the tops and bottoms securely. Lay the pasties on a baking-parchment-lined baking tray, seam side down, and make a steam hole in the top. Brush over with beaten egg and decorate as lavishly as the pastry trimmings allow. Bake until the pastry is golden brown, about 40 to 45 minutes.

The remaining juices can be reheated and handed round separately, with a dash of lemon juice added. Red-currant jelly is very good with venison.

Serves 6

Stooking turf on the Glenbeigh Road, Co. Kerry

BEEF AND MUSHROOM PIE WITH GUINNESS

Leg of beef is a good choice for dishes of this type, for, although it takes a long time to cook initially, it remains tender and juicy.

2 pounds beef stew meat, cubed

2 tablespoons all-purpose flour

2 tablespoons olive oil

2 large onions, chopped

1 carrot, chopped

1 celery stick, chopped

bouquet garni of 1 bay leaf, 1 fresh thyme sprig, and 1 fresh parsley sprig, tied with string

4 canned anchovies, drained

2 cups Guinness ale

3 cups mushrooms

8 ounce puff pastry dough

1 egg, beaten

salt and freshly ground black pepper

Toss the beef in the flour and brown in the oil in a large saucepan. Add the onions, carrot, celery, the bouquet garni, and seasoning. Mash the anchovies and stir in. Pour the Guinness over the top, stir well, cover, and cook very slowly until the meat is almost tender, about 1½ hours. (This can be done in the oven, if preferred.)

Add the mushrooms and continue cooking for 25 minutes longer. Leave to cool.

Preheat the oven to 375°F. Transfer the contents of the saucepan to a deep baking dish with a flat rim or ceramic pie dish. Adjust the seasoning.

Roll out the dough on a floured board, until you have a large circle about 1½ inches larger than the dish. Cut off the surplus in a long strip and press onto the dampened edge of the dish. Lay the remaining dough circle over the pie, pressing onto the strip to attach it securely. Crimp the edges decoratively. Make a vent in the middle and decorate the pie with leaves or flowers made from the dough trimmings. Brush with the beaten egg. Bake until the pastry is risen and golden.

Serve with really creamy mashed potatoes, made with plenty of butter and milk and dusted over with parsley.

Serves 6

Ballyduff potato pickers, Co. Kerry

STUFFED PORK CHOPS WITH POTATO-APPLE FRITTERS

4 loin chops, 1-inch thick
1 tablespoon balsamic
  vinegar
grated zest and juice of
  1 lemon
1 tablespoon Dijon mustard
chopped fresh parsley
1 cup fresh whole-wheat
  bread crumbs
finely chopped fresh thyme
3 tablespoons butter
1 tablespoon grated fresh
  gingerroot, peeled
1 apple, peeled, cored, and
  finely chopped
1 egg, beaten
²/₃ cup hard cider, white
  wine, or chicken stock
1 tablespoon oil
salt and freshly ground
  black pepper

FOR THE FRITTERS
1¹/₂ cups grated raw potato
1 cup grated apple
¹/₃ cup all-purpose flour
2 eggs
2 tablespoons whipping cream
oil and butter for frying
salt

Make cuts in the fat along the edge of the chops at ¹/₂-inch intervals (this helps the fat to cook and prevents the chops from curling during cooking). Make a horizontal incision in the side of each chop to form a pocket. Mix the vinegar, lemon juice, and mustard together. Toss the chops in this mixture. Leave to marinate while you make the stuffing, or longer, if time allows.

Put the parsley in a bowl with the lemon zest, bread crumbs, and thyme. Melt 1 tablespoon butter in a large skillet. Add the ginger and fry for a few moments. Add the apple and cook until soft. Stir in the bread crumbs and season well. Bind with the beaten egg. Spoon the stuffing into the pockets in the chops and secure with wooden toothpicks.

Add half the remaining butter and the oil to the pan and, turning up the heat, brown the chops well on each side. Add the cider, wine, or stock and the remaining marinade. Cover the pan, lower the heat, and simmer until the chops are cooked through, 10 to 12 minutes. Transfer the chops to a serving dish and keep warm.

Add the remaining butter to the pan, scrape up the residue, and bubble for a few moments to reduce. Adjust the seasoning and pour over the chops; keep warm while you make the fritters.

Mix the potato and apples together with the flour. Bind with the eggs and cream and mix to a batter consistency. Fry, 1 tablespoon at a time, in hot oil and butter. Drain and sprinkle with salt.

Serves 4

BREAST OF CHICKEN
WITH WALNUTS AND APPLE

On rainy days alone I dine,
Upon a chick, and pint of wine.
On rainy days I dine alone,
And pick my chicken to the bone.
Jonathan Swift

4 tablespoons butter
¹/₂ large cooking apple, such
as Bramley or Courtlands,
peeled and chopped
4 fresh sage leaves, finely
chopped, or a tiny pinch of
dried sage
³/₄ cup walnuts, chopped
4 large chicken breasts, halved
2 tablespoons all-purpose
flour
1 egg, beaten
³/₄ cup dry bread crumbs
1 tablespoon oil
²/₃ cup heavy cream or
crème fraîche
paprika, salt, and freshly
ground black pepper

In a small saucepan, melt 1
tablespoon of butter. Add the
apple, sage, and walnuts. Cook
slowly until the apple is just
beginning to soften and the
walnuts beginning to color; set
aside to cool. Season well.

Make a long, deep incision in
the sides of the chicken breasts,
cutting lengthwise to make a
deep pocket. Divide the stuffing
between the chicken breasts,
pushing it well into the pockets.
Season and flour the chicken,
then dip in the egg and roll in
bread crumbs. Secure with
wooden toothpicks. (If the chicken
is being prepared in advance, chill
the stuffing before inserting it.)

In a large skillet, melt 2
tablespoons butter with the oil.
Add the chicken breasts and fry
over medium heat, turning once
or twice, until cooked and golden,
but still moist, 5 to 7 minutes on
each side, depending on thickness.

Remove the chicken from the
pan and keep warm. Wipe any
burnt crumbs from the pan with
paper towels. Pour in the cream.
Add any remaining stuffing or
crumbs, season well with salt,
pepper, and paprika and bubble
up for a few moments, scraping
up the sediment. Whisk in the
remaining butter and pour over
the chicken.

Serves 4

Dingle Bay, Co. Kerry

ROAST TURKEY

This traditional turkey has two stuffings and is semi-braised, to retain moisture.

12 pound turkey

4 tablespoons butter

2 large onions, halved

8 cloves

2 carrots, coarsely chopped

2 celery sticks, coarsely
chopped

8 ounce slab bacon, rind
removed and cut in strips

1¼ cups hard cider or
white wine

1 tablespoon all-purpose flour

salt and freshly ground
black pepper

FOR THE PRUNE-AND-
CHICKEN LIVER STUFFING

1 large onion, finely chopped

4 tablespoons butter

8 ounce chicken livers,
cleaned and chopped

6 cups fresh bread crumbs

1 celery stick, finely chopped

1 carrot, grated

1½ cups pitted and chopped
prunes

small glass vermouth or
sherry

2 teaspoons Italian seasoning

1 teaspoon ground mace

salt and freshly ground
black pepper

FOR THE APPLE-AND-
WALNUT STUFFING

1½ cups chopped walnuts

2 cooking apples, peeled and
chopped

4 tablespoons butter, softened

1 tablespoon grated fresh
peeled gingerroot

1 cup fresh bread crumbs

salt and freshly ground
black pepper

To make the prune stuffing, cook the onion in half the butter. Add the livers and cook until slightly pink. Add to the bread crumbs. In the remaining butter, cook the celery, carrot, and prunes for a few minutes. Stir in the vermouth or sherry, herbs, and mace. Season to taste. Bubble up well. Pour into the bread crumb mixture and mix well. Leave to cool.

Preheat the oven to 450°F.

To make the apple stuffing, mix all the ingredients together and season well.

Stuff the turkey's body cavity loosely with the prune stuffing. Insert slices of butter under the breast skin. Skewer or tie the legs together. Stuff the crop with the apple stuffing and seal with a skewer. Season the turkey thoroughly and rub the breast well with butter.

Put the onions, stuck with the cloves, in a deep roasting pan with the vegetables, bacon, and cider. Lay the turkey on its side on top.

Put the turkey in the oven and immediately lower the heat to 350°F. After 45 minutes, turn the turkey onto the other side and baste well. After 45 minutes longer, turn the turkey breast-side up and continue roasting 45 minutes to 1 hour, basting well and covering the breast with foil if it is browning too fast. Test the

turkey is cooked by inserting a skewer between the thigh and the breast; the juices should be clear. Transfer the turkey to a serving platter and cover with foil and a towel; leave to relax the meat and keep it juicy. It will stay warm for 45 minutes to an hour.

To make the gravy, strain the stock from the roasting pan and leave it to stand so the fat rises to the top. Remove the fat and set it aside. Mix 1 tablespoon flour with 1 tablespoon of the reserved fat in a saucepan. Blend in the stock. Boil hard to thicken slightly and reduce. Pour into a sauceboat and serve very hot.

Crisp bacon rolls and sausages can be used to garnish the dish and rowanberry or cranberry jelly can be handed separately. The prune stuffing can be baked separately if preferred.

Serves 8 to 10

Conor Pass, Co. Kerry

GRATIN OF PARSNIPS AND PEARS

"Fair words butter no parsnips"
Old saying.
This is a simple and delicious recipe which can be prepared in advance and finished when required.

3 to 4 large parsnips
3 large pears
1 tablespoon lemon juice
4 tablespoons butter
$^1/_4$ cup stale bread crumbs
salt and freshly ground
** black pepper**
grated nutmeg

Preheat the oven to 350°F. Cut the parsnips in quarters lengthwise and cut away some of the hard cores, then peel, trim and cut into chunks. Peel and core the pears and chop roughly.

Put the parsnips and pears in a large saucepan. Add salt and lemon juice and just barely cover with water. Boil until tender. Drain well and mash with the butter until creamy, adding pepper to taste and a grating of nutmeg.

Transfer to a baking dish suitable for serving from. Sprinkle the bread crumbs over the top. Bake 15 to 20 minutes or until golden brown.

Serves 6

ORANGE, CELERY, AND WATERCRESS SALAD

This winter salad is the classic partner for wild duck. It is equally good with tame fowl and pork. Corn salad or arugula, in season, can also be used.

2 to 3 oranges
6 to 8 celery sticks, finely sliced
1 to 2 bunches watercress
1 small onion, finely chopped
2 tablespoons olive oil
1 tablespoon lemon juice
salt and paprika

Peel the oranges, removing as much pith as possible. Rinse and gently shake the watercress dry. Arrange on a flat dish, with the celery. Slice the oranges thinly and arrange on top, removing any seeds.

Sprinkle the onion over the oranges and season with salt. Dress the salad with oil and lemon only when ready to serve and sprinkle a little paprika over the top.

Serves 6

Cloghane on the Dingle Peninsula

WINTER
miscellaneous

CHRISTMAS CHUTNEY

2 pounds cooking apples, such
  as Bramley or Courtlands
2¹/₂ cups finely chopped
  onions
1¹/₄ cups white-wine
  or malt vinegar
heaping 1 cup sugar
¹/₃ cup brown sugar
8 ounce mixed nuts, such as
  chestnuts, walnuts, and
  almonds
2 teaspoons ground ginger
grated zest and juice of
  1 lemon
1 teaspoon salt

Peel, core, and chop the apples.
Cook the onions in the vinegar,
until soft. Add the apples and
cook 3 to 4 minutes. Stir in the
remaining ingredients and simmer
slowly until the mixture begins to
thicken, lowering the heat and
stirring frequently to prevent it
from burning.

Pour into warm, sterilized jars
with plastic-lined lids.

Chutneys improve with keeping,
the flavors becoming subtler after
about 2 to 3 months. If the
chutney is made for immediate
use, wine vinegar is best, as malt
vinegar needs time to mellow.

Fills about 5 x ³/₄-pint jars

A warm corner

ROWAN JELLY

The rowan tree, or mountain ash, like the elder tree, had important magical properties for our Celtic ancestors. The red berries make an excellent jelly for game, hams, and pâtés, the flavor maturing as it ages. Rowan jelly can be used instead of red-currant jelly in sauces and with lamb. If rowans are unavailable, use cranberries.

3 pounds rowans
2 large cooking apples, such
  as Bramley or Courtlands,
  coarsely chopped
grated zest and juice of
  1 lemon
sugar

Put the rowans in a saucepan and crush them slightly. Add the coarsely chopped apples (no need to peel or core) and lemon zest. Just cover with water and cook until both are very soft. Strain overnight through a jelly bag. (An old linen dish towel over a large plastic colander can be used.)

Measure the juice collected and place in a large saucepan or preserving pan. Add the lemon juice, and 2¼ cups sugar for each 2½ cups of liquid. Stir over low heat to dissolve the sugar. Increase the heat and boil hard until a few drops on a chilled saucer will wrinkle when pressed with a finger. Pot into hot, sterilized jars.

LONGFORD CAKES

These delicious mouthfuls are simple to make for afternoon tea. Made in 4-inch tartlet pans, they make a very good dessert.

FOR THE PASTRY

2 cups all-purpose flour, sifted

1 tablespoon superfine sugar

³/₄ cup butter

2 egg yolks

1 to 2 tablespoons cold water

salt

FOR THE FILLING

2 tablespoons blanched almonds, very finely ground

5 tablespoons apricot jam

scant 1 cup coarsely chopped walnuts

5 tablespoons golden raisins

2 tablespoons very finely chopped apple

1 tablespoon grated lemon zest

1 egg, beaten, to glaze

sugar, to decorate

FOR THE GERANIUM CREAM

2 to 3 scented geranium leaves

1 cup heavy cream, whipped

To make the pastry dough, mix together the flour, sugar, and a pinch of salt. Rub in the butter, and then moisten with the egg yolks, adding 1 tablespoon or so cold water as required. Chill at least 30 minutes.

Preheat the oven to 375°F. Grease and line six 4-inch tartlet pans. Roll out the pastry very thinly and line the pans, gathering the trimmings and rerolling to make the lids.

Mix all the filling ingredients together, chopping finely any large pieces of apricot in the jam. Divide between the tartlets.

Dampen the dough edges and put on the lids, press well together to seal and tidy up the edges. Glaze with the beaten egg, make vents in the tops and sprinkle with sugar. Bake 25 to 30 minutes, until the pastry is golden brown.

Serve with geranium cream, made as follows: rinse and dry the scented geranium leaves and infuse in the cream for several hours.

Makes 6 tartlets

A BOWL OF BISHOP

This was the favourite "night-cap" of the eighteenth century, famed in song and verse. Jonathan Swift wrote about it, although when Stella made it for him, the oranges were roasted in front of the fire, and the wine heated with a hot poker.

4 oranges
20 cloves
1 cinnamon stick
2 to 3 pieces mace
1 teaspoon allspice berries
2¹/₂ cups water
bottle ruby port
sugar lumps or sugar
1 nutmeg
juice of 1 lemon

Preheat the oven to 350°F. Make incisions in 2 of the oranges and press the cloves into them. Roast for half an hour or so, until they make a slightly hissing sound.

Put the whole spices in the water in a saucepan (if you can't get whole mace, use a nutmeg or more allspice berries) and boil until reduced by half. In another saucepan, heat the port, then ignite it to burn off some of the alcohol and concentrate the flavor. (If you can't bear to do this, ignore it!)

Put the port, spiced water, and roasted oranges into a large bowl, ideally one which can be kept warm. Stir in sugar to taste. Slice the remaining oranges into the bowl, grate in some nutmeg, and sharpen the flavor with lemon juice.

Makes about 8 glasses

Longford Cakes and a Bowl of Bishop

WINTER
desserts

CHRISTMAS PLUM PUDDING

While today's taste is for lighter food, an exception is always made in favor of the traditional Christmas plum pudding, although it, too, is evolving—butter is widely used today instead of suet and there hasn't been any meat in it for almost a hundred years.

1¹/₃ cups candied cherries

8 ounce candied citrus peel

³/₄ cup each shelled walnuts and blanched almonds

6 cups fresh bread crumbs

¹/₃ cup all-purpose flour

1 cup plus 2 tablespoons light brown sugar

1 large apple, peeled and chopped

1¹/₃ cups each raisins, currants, and golden raisins

1 tablespoon apple-pie spice

1¹/₂ cups (3 sticks) butter or 1¹/₂ cups shredded suet

8 eggs

large glass Irish whiskey or sherry

³/₄ cup Guinness ale

salt

Cut the cherries in half. Thinly slice the citrus peel and then chop it finely. Chop the nuts coarsely. Mix all the fruit together with the bread crumbs, flour, sugar, apple, dried fruit, apple-pie spice, and a pinch of salt. Add the suet, if it is being used.

Soften the butter, if using, and gradually beat the eggs into it with the whiskey or sherry. Pour this mixture into the dry ingredients and mix well. Add enough of the Guinness to make a dropping texture but don't make it too runny.

Place circles of baking parchment in the bottoms of two 3³/₄ cup heatproof bowls or traditional Irish pudding basins; butter them well. Fill the bowls two-thirds full, to leave room for expansion. Cover the tops with

more buttered paper and then cover well with foil. The puddings will take 5 to 6 hours steaming. They can also be cooked at a low heat in the oven, by standing the bowls in a pan of water and enclosing both pan and bowl completely in foil, making a steamproof tent, for 5¹/₂ hours at 300°F.

When cooked, leave to cool before removing the foil. Cover with fresh baking parchment and more foil before storing in a cool place until required. The puddings require steaming 1¹/₂ to 2 hours further before they are eaten.

Note: the puddings can be left overnight in the refrigerator before steaming, if it's not convenient to cook them immediately.

Each pudding serves 6

PEARS POACHED IN WHITE WINE

¹/₂ cup sugar
2 cinnamon sticks
grated zest of 1 small orange
bottle sweet white wine,
  such as Muscatel
6 pears
1 tablespoon lemon juice
grated nutmeg, to decorate

Put the sugar, cinnamon sticks, orange zest, and wine in a saucepan which will just hold the pears upright. Heat the liquid slowly until the sugar dissolves, then boil hard for a few minutes.

Peel the pears carefully, leaving the stalks on and brushing each with lemon juice. Trim the bottoms slightly so they stand upright. Poach in the wine for about 15 minutes, or until they are tender but not too soft. If there is insufficient liquid to come up to the stalks, add water.

When the pears are cooked, remove and leave to cool. Take the cinnamon sticks out of the poaching liquid and boil the liquid hard, uncovered, until it forms a thin syrup. Leave to cool. Pour the syrup over the pears and grate a little nutmeg over the top before serving.

Serves 6

Sunset on the Dingle Peninsula

COFFEE-WALNUT
ICE CREAM

1^1/$_4$ **cups milk**
5 tablespoons freshly ground
  coffee
2^1/$_2$ **cups whipping cream**
7 egg yolks
^{3}/$_4$ **cups plus 2 tablespoons**
  sugar
scant 1 cup walnuts
2 tablespoons rum

Bring the milk to a boil. Stir in the
coffee and leave to infuse 30
minutes. Strain the milk and stir
the cream into it. Beat the egg
yolks and sugar together until
pale and creamy. Gradually beat
in the milk. Return to the
saucepan and cook over low heat
until the custard thickens slightly
and coats the back of a spoon; do
not allow to boil. Leave to cool.

  Chop the walnuts finely and stir
into the custard, with the rum.
Freeze in the usual manner by
taking the mixture out and
beating well 2 to 3 times during
freezing, to prevent the formation
of ice particles.

  Serve in glasses with Cats'
Tongues or similar little cookies.
  Serves 4 to 6

CATS'
TONGUES

6 tablespoons butter, softened
^{1}/$_3$ **cup superfine sugar**
3 egg whites
^{1}/$_2$ **all-purpose flour, sifted**

Preheat the oven to 400°F.
Cream the butter and sugar
together until pale and creamy.
Add the unbeaten egg whites.
Mix well, and then gradually fold
in the flour.

  Line 2 trays with baking
parchment. Pipe the dough into
little strips 2 inches long and
about ^{1}/$_4$-inch wide. Bake 6 to 8
minutes until brown at the edges.
Transfer with a spatula to a rack
to cool.
  Makes 20 to 25

Mountain lakes in the Conor Pass

WINTER
baking

SODA BREAD WITH ONIONS

*This variation on classic Irish soda bread is good with
potted meats and pâtés.*

4 tablespoons olive oil
1 large onion, finely chopped
3¹/₃ cups white bread flour
¹/₂ teaspoon salt
1 teaspoon baking soda
2¹/₂ cups buttermilk
2 teaspoons caraway seeds

Preheat the oven to 350°F. Heat
1 tablespoon of the oil in a heavy
saucepan. Add the onions and
cook until they are dark brown
and crisp but not burned; cool.

Sift the flour and salt together.
Dissolve the baking soda in 1
tablespoon buttermilk. Add this,
with the remaining 3 tablespoons
olive oil, to the remaining
buttermilk. Add the onions and
seeds to the flour. Make a well in
the middle and add the liquid.
Using a fork, mix it all together
thoroughly, mixing lightly until you
have a fairly smooth texture.
Using floured hands, shape the
mixture into a round cake. Cut a
cross in the top and transfer to a
greased baking sheet. Bake until
the loaf gives a hollow sound
when tapped on the bottom,
about 40 minutes.

Note: if buttermilk is not
available, combine fresh milk and
2 teaspoons baking powder.

A film set from the film Far and Away, *Co. Kerry*
Overleaf: Garrettstown Strand, Courtmacsherry Bay, Co. Cork

QUEEN OF PUDDINGS

Here is a lighter version of this favorite, which pleases all ages.

5 eggs
2 cups whipping cream
1¼ cups milk
small piece cinnamon stick
1 teaspoon grated lemon zest
1 teaspoon vanilla extract
2 tablespoons sugar,
  for the pudding
1½ cups fresh bread crumbs
4 to 5 tablespoons raspberry
  jam
¾ cup plus 2 tablespoons
  sugar, for the meringue

Separate 3 of the eggs; set whites aside for meringue. Beat the remaining eggs and yolks together with the cream, milk, flavorings, and 2 tablespoons sugar. Put the bread crumbs in a baking dish suitable for serving from. Pour the cream mixture over them and infuse in the refrigerator for several hours.

Preheat the oven to 325°F. Bake the pudding 15 to 20 minutes until set. Leave to cool for a few minutes, then spread the jam over the surface.

Raise the heat to 375°F. Beat the egg whites until they form stiff peaks. Sprinkle 6 tablespoons of the sugar in slowly, whisking continuously. Fold in the remaining sugar thoroughly. Spread the meringue over the jam completely. Bake 15 minutes until meringue is set and brown, being careful it doesn't burn.

Serves 6

index